Edward de Bono was born in Malta and after his initial education at St Edward's College, Malta, and the Royal University of Malta, where he obtained a degree in medicine, he proceeded as a Rhodes Scholar to Christ Church, Oxford, where he gained an honours degree in psychology and physiology and then a D.Phil. in medicine. He also holds a Ph.D. from Cambridge. He has had faculty appointments at the universities of Oxford, London, Cambridge and Harvard.

Dr de Bono runs the largest curriculum programme for the direct teaching of thinking in schools. Some countries, like Venezuela, have made it compulsory in all schools, and there is a growing use in Canada, the USA, China and the USSR. Dr de Bono's instruction in thinking has also been sought by such well-known corporations as NTT (Japan), Du Pont, Ericsson, United Technologies, American Standard, Exxon and Shell. His 'Six Hats' method is now used in many corporations, such as Prudential and IBM. He has also worked for governments, including the Government of California on toxic waste problems. He may be teaching senior executives of multinational corporations one day and nine-year-olds in a primary school the next.

Dr de Bono has been invited to address such meetings as The Institute of Institutional Investors, The Commonwealth Law Conference, The American Bar Association, The World Congress on Emergency and Disaster Medicine, The World Economic Forum (Davos) and The Society of Information Managers. In 1989 he chaired a meeting of Nobel Prize laureates in Seoul, Korea.

He is the founder and director of the Cognitive Research Trust (1969) and the Centre for the Study of Thinking and the founder of SITO (Supranational Independent Thinking Organisation) which was set up as a sort of intellectual Red Cross to provide additional and creative thinking on problems and issues. He has also set up a Task Force on Thinking in Washington.

Dr de Bono has been invited to lecture and work in forty-five countries. He has written over thirty books and there are translations available in twenty-four languages, including Chinese, Korean, Japanese, Russian, Arabic, Hebrew, Urdu, Bahasa and all major languages. He has made two television series, 'De Bono's Course in Thinking' for the BBC and 'The Greatest Thinkers' for WDR, Germany. He runs a newsletter which is published ten times a year and is the inventor of the classic L-Game which is said to be the simplest real game ever invented. He is perhaps best known for originating the term 'lateral thinking', which now has an entry in the Oxford English Dictionary.

Other titles published by Penguin:

Atlas of Management Thinking
Children Solve Problems
Conflicts: A Better Way to Resolve Them
The Five-Day Course in Thinking
Future Positive
The Happiness Purpose
Lateral Thinking for Management
Letters to Thinkers
The Mechanism of the Mind
Opportunities
Po: Beyond Yes and No
Practical Thinking
Six Thinking Hats
Teaching Thinking
The Use of Lateral Thinking
Wordpower

and forthcoming:

I Am Right You Are Wrong

Edward de Bono

Lateral Thinking

A Textbook of Creativity

Penguin Books

PENGUIN BOOKS

Published by the Penguin Group
Penguin Books Ltd, 27 Wrights Lane, London W8 5TZ, England
Viking Penguin, a division of Penguin Books USA Inc.
375 Hudson Street, New York, New York 10014, USA
Penguin Books Australia Ltd, Ringwood, Victoria, Australia
Penguin Books Canada Ltd, 2801 John Street, Markham, Ontario, Canada L3R 1B4
Penguin Books (NZ) Ltd, 182–190 Wairau Road, Auckland 10, New Zealand

Penguin Books Ltd, Registered Offices: Harmondsworth, Middlesex, England

First published by Ward Lock Education 1970
Published in Pelican Books 1977
Reprinted in Penguin Books 1990
10 9 8 7 6 5 4 3 2 1

Made and printed in Great Britain by
BPCC Hazell Books
Aylesbury, Bucks, England
Member of BPCC Ltd.
Set in Linotype Juliana

Contents

7   Preface
9   Introduction
15   Use of this book
25   The way the mind works
37   Difference between lateral and vertical thinking
44   Attitudes towards lateral thinking
48   Basic nature of lateral thinking
52   The use of lateral thinking
56   Techniques
58   The generation of alternatives
82   Challenging assumptions
93   Innovation
95   Suspended judgement
100   Design
108   Dominant ideas and crucial factors
116   Fractionation
124   The reversal method
131   Brainstorming
147   Analogies
154   Choice of entry point and attention area
169   Random stimulation
181   Concepts/divisions/polarization
196   The new word po
231   Blocked by openness
240   Description/problem solving/design
258   Summary

Preface

This book is intended for use both at home and at school. At school the emphasis has traditionally always been on vertical thinking which is effective but incomplete. This selective type of thinking needs to be supplemented with the generative qualities of creative thinking. This is beginning to happen in some schools but even so creativity is usually treated as something desirable which is to be brought about by vague exhortation. There is no deliberate and practical procedure for bringing it about. This book is about lateral thinking which is the process of using information to bring about creativity and insight restructuring. Lateral thinking can be learned, practised and used. It is possible to acquire skill in it just as it is possible to acquire skill in mathematics.

The book should be of use to teachers who are looking for a practical way to handle this type of thinking which is becoming ever more important. The book provides formal opportunities to practise lateral thinking and also an explanation of the processes involved. The teacher may either use the book for his or her own interest or, better still, as a basis for classroom work.

Since the universal introduction of practical creativity into school education may take some time to come about, parents might not wish to wait for this. They might prefer to supplement the school situation with home instruction in lateral thinking.

It is emphasized that there is no antagonism between the two sorts of thinking. Both are necessary. Vertical thinking is immensely useful but one needs to enhance its usefulness by adding creativity and tempering its rigidity. Eventually this will be done at school but until that time it may be necessary to do it at home.

*

The book is not intended to be read through at one sitting but worked through slowly – over months or even years. For that reason many of the principles are repeated at intervals throughout the book in order to hold the subject together and prevent it fragmenting into mere techniques. In using the book it is important to remember that practice is far more important than understanding of the process.

Introduction

Lateral thinking is closely related to insight, creativity and humour. All four processes have the same basis. But whereas insight, creativity and humour can only be prayed for, lateral thinking is a more deliberate process. It is as definite a way of using the mind as logical thinking – but a very different way.

Culture is concerned with establishing ideas. Education is concerned with communicating those established ideas. Both are concerned with improving ideas by bringing them up to date. The only available method for changing ideas is conflict which works in two ways. In the first way there is a head on confrontation between opposing ideas. One or other of the ideas achieves a practical dominance over the other idea which is suppressed but not changed. In the second way there is a conflict between new information and the old idea. As a result of this conflict the old idea is supposed to be changed. This is the method of science which is always seeking to generate new information to upset the old ideas and bring about new ones. It is more than the method of science – it is the method of human knowledge.

Education is based on the safe assumption that one only has to go on collecting more and more information for it to sort itself into useful ideas. We have developed tools for handling the information: mathematics for extending it, logical thinking for refining it.

The conflict method for changing ideas works well where the information can be evaluated in some objective manner. But the method does not work at all when the new information can only be evaluated through the old idea. Instead of being changed the old idea is strengthened and made ever more rigid.

The most effective way of changing ideas is not from outside by conflict but from within by the insight rearrangement of available information. Insight is the only effective way of changing ideas in a myth situation – when information cannot be evaluated objectively. Even when information can be evaluated objectively, as in science, an insight rearrangement of information leads to huge leaps forward. Education is not only concerned with collecting information but also with the best ways of using information that has been collected.

When ideas lead information rather than lag behind progress is rapid. Yet we have developed no practical tools for handling insight. We can only go on collecting information and hope that at some stage it will come about. Lateral thinking is an insight tool.

Insight, creativity and humour are so elusive because the mind is so efficient. The mind functions to create patterns out of its surroundings. Once the patterns are formed it becomes possible to recognize them, to react to them, to use them. As the patterns are used they become ever more firmly established.

The pattern using system is a very efficient way of handling information. Once established the patterns form a sort of code. The advantage of a code system is that instead of having to collect all the information one collects just enough to identify the code pattern which is then called forth even as library books on a particular subject are called forth by a catalogue code number.

It is convenient to talk of the mind as if it were some information handling machine – perhaps like a computer. The mind is not a machine, however, but a special environment which allows information to organize itself into patterns. This self-organizing, self-maximizing, memory system is very good at creating patterns and that is the effectiveness of mind.

But inseparable from the great usefulness of a patterning system are certain limitations. In such a system it is easy to combine patterns or to add to them but it is extremely difficult to restructure them for the patterns control attention. Insight and humour both involve the restructuring of patterns. Creativity also involves restructuring but with more emphasis on the escape from restricting patterns. Lateral thinking involves restructuring, escape and the provocation of new patterns.

Lateral thinking is closely related to creativity. But whereas creativity is too often only the description of a result, lateral thinking is the description of a process. One can only admire a result but one can learn to use a process. There is about creativity a mystique of talent and intangibles. This may be justified in the art world where creativity involves aesthetic sensibility, emotional resonance and a gift for expression. But it is not justified outside that world. More and more creativity is coming to be valued as the essential ingredient in change and in progress. It is coming to be valued above knowledge and above technique since both these are becoming so accessible. In order to be able to use creativity one must rid it of this aura of mystique and regard it as a way of using the mind – a way of handling information. This is what lateral thinking is about.

Lateral thinking is concerned with the generation of new ideas. There is a curious notion that new ideas have to do with technical invention. This is a very minor aspect of the matter. New ideas are the stuff of change and progress in every field from science to art, from politics to personal happiness.

Lateral thinking is also concerned with breaking out of the concept prisons of old ideas. This leads to changes in attitude and approach; to looking in a different way at things which have always been looked at in the same way. Liberation from old ideas and the stimulation of new ones are twin aspects of lateral thinking.

Lateral thinking is quite distinct from vertical thinking which is the traditional type of thinking. In vertical thinking one moves forward by sequential steps each of which must be justified. The distinction between the two sorts of thinking is sharp. For instance in lateral thinking one uses information not for its own sake but for its effect. In lateral thinking one may have to be wrong at some stage in order to achieve a correct solution; in vertical thinking (logic or mathematics) this would be impossible. In lateral thinking one may deliberately seek out irrelevant information; in vertical thinking one selects out only what is relevant.

Lateral thinking is not a substitute for vertical thinking. Both are required. They are complementary. Lateral thinking is generative. Vertical thinking is selective.

With vertical thinking one may reach a conclusion by a valid series of steps. Because of the soundness of the steps one is arrogantly certain of the correctness of the conclusion. But no matter how correct the path may be the starting point was a matter of perceptual choice which fashioned the basic concepts used. For instance perceptual choice tends to create sharp divisions and use extreme polarization. Vertical thinking would then work on the concepts produced in this manner. Lateral thinking is needed to handle the perceptual choice which is itself beyond the reach of vertical thinking. Lateral thinking would also temper the arrogance of any rigid conclusion no matter how soundly it appeared to have been worked out.

Lateral thinking enhances the effectiveness of vertical thinking. Vertical thinking develops the ideas generated by lateral thinking. You cannot dig a hole in a different place by digging the same hole deeper. Vertical thinking is used to dig the same hole deeper. Lateral thinking is used to dig a hole in a different place.

The exclusive emphasis on vertical thinking in the past makes it all the more necessary to teach lateral thinking. It is not just that vertical thinking alone is insufficient for progress but that by itself it can be dangerous.

Like logical thinking lateral thinking is a way of using the mind. It is a habit of mind and an attitude of mind. There are specific techniques that can be used just as there are specific techniques in logical thinking. There is some emphasis on techniques in this book not because they are an important part of lateral thinking but because they are practical. Goodwill and exhortation are not enough to develop skill in lateral thinking. One needs an actual setting in which to practise and some tangible techniques with which to practise. From an understanding of the techniques, and from fluency in their use, lateral thinking develops as an attitude of mind. One can also make practical use of the techniques.

Lateral thinking is not some magic new system. There have always been instances where people have used lateral thinking to produce some result. There have always been people who tended naturally towards lateral thinking. The purpose of this book is to show that lateral thinking is a very basic part of thinking and that one can develop some skill in it. Instead of just hoping for insight and creativity one can use lateral thinking in a deliberate and practical manner.

Summary

The purpose of thinking is to collect information and to make the best possible use of it. Because of the way the mind works to create fixed concept patterns we cannot make the best use of new information unless we have some means for restructuring the old patterns and bringing them up to date. Our traditional methods of thinking teach us how to refine such patterns and establish their validity. But we shall always make less than the best use of available information unless we know how to create new patterns and escape from the dominance of the old ones. Vertical thinking is concerned with proving or developing concept patterns. Lateral thinking is concerned with restructuring such patterns (insight) and provoking new ones (creativity). Lateral and vertical thinking are complementary. Skill in both is necessary. Yet the emphasis in education has always been exclusively on vertical thinking.

The need for lateral thinking arises from the limitations of the behaviour of mind as a self-maximizing memory system.

Use of this book

This book is not intended to introduce a new subject nor is it intended to acquaint the reader with what is happening in a certain field. The book is meant to be used. It is meant to be used by the reader for his own sake and through the teacher for the sake of the students.

Age

The processes described in this book are basic ones. They apply to all ages and to all different levels of learning. I have used some of the most elementary demonstrations on the most sophisticated of groups such as advanced computer programmers and they have not felt that they were wasting their time. The more sophisticated the group the better is it able to abstract the process from the particular form in which it is demonstrated. While the lower age groups enjoy the item for its own sake the older age groups look more closely at the point behind it. Although the simpler items are applicable to all age groups the more complicated items may only be of use to more senior groups.

In the younger age groups the visual form is much more effective than the verbal since a child can always attempt to express something visually and, more importantly, to understand something that has been expressed visually.

From the age of seven right up to and through university education the lateral thinking process is relevant. This may seem a wide age group but the process is as basic as logical thinking and clearly the relevance of this is not limited to a particular age group. In a similar manner the relevance of lateral thinking cuts across the distinctions of subject even more than does mathematics. Lateral thinking is relevant whether one is studying science or engineering or history or English. It is because of this general application that the material used in this book does not require the background of any particular subject.

An attempt should be made to develop lateral thinking attitudes as a habit of mind at least from the age of seven onwards. The actual application of the ideas expressed in this book to a particular age level must depend to some extent on the experience of the teacher in presenting the material in an appropriate form. The two usual mistakes in this regard are:

● To assume that it is obvious and that everyone thinks laterally anyway.

● To assume that it is rather a special subject and not of use or relevance to everyone.

The practical aspect of the book does get more complex as one proceeds through the book (this is apart from the background material intended for the teacher). In general the first part of the practical material is suitable for seven-year-olds and the later parts are suitable for anyone. This is not to imply that the first part is only suitable for young children or the later parts are only suitable for adults but that there is a way of putting over the lateral thinking attitude to any age group.

Format

Like logical thinking, lateral thinking is a general attitude of mind which may make use of certain techniques on occasion. Nevertheless this attitude of mind can best be taught in a formal setting using specific material and exercises. This is to encourage the development of the lateral thinking habit. Without a formal setting one is reduced to mere encouragement and the appreciation of lateral thinking when it occurs – neither of which processes do much to develop the habit.

To set aside a definite period for teaching lateral thinking is much more use than trying to gently introduce its principles in the course of teaching some other subject.

If one has to teach it along with some other subject then one should set aside a short, defined period as part of the general period (even though the subject matter may be the same as for the rest of the period).

A one hour period every week throughout education would be quite sufficient to bring about the lateral thinking attitude – or the creative attitude if you prefer to call it that.

The practical parts of the book are separated into different aspects. It is not suggested that one should work through the book taking a section at each lesson and then passing on to the next section. This would be quite useless. Instead one uses the basic structure of each section over and over again until one is thoroughly familiar with the process. One may spend several sessions on a particular section or even several months. All the time one is changing the basic material but developing the same lateral thinking process. It is the use of lateral thinking that counts, not knowledge of each and every process. One can develop the lateral attitude of mind as easily through thorough practice in one technique as through brief practice in them all.

There is nothing special about the techniques. It is the attitude behind them that counts. But mere exhortation and goodwill are not enough. If one is to develop a skill one must have some formal setting in which to practise it – and some tools to use. The best way to acquire skill in lateral thinking is to acquire skill in the use of a collection of tools which are all used to bring about the same effect.

Materials

Many of the demonstrations used in this book may seem trivial and artificial. They are. The demonstrations are used in order to make clear some point about the thinking process. They are not intended to teach anything but to encourage the reader to develop some insight into the natural behaviour of the mind. Just as the actual content of parables or fables is so much less important than the point they are intended to convey so the demonstrations may be trivial in content in order to make an important point.

There is unfortunately no switch in the mind which can be flicked one way for dealing with all important matters and the other way for dealing with minor matters.

Whatever the importance of the matter the system behaves in the same way, that is according to its nature. In important matters the working of the system may be distorted by emotional considerations which do not interfere with the handling of trivial matters. The only effect is to make the working worse than it can be. *Hence the defects of the system in dealing with trivial matters are at least the same defects which will be present when dealing with more important matters.*

It is the process not the product that matters. The trivial and artificial items illustrate the process in a neat and accessible manner. The process can be extracted just as the relationships expressed in a formula in algebra can be separated from what the symbols actually stand for.

Many of the items are visual and even geometric. This is deliberate because the use of verbal illustrations can be misleading. Words are already neat and fixed packages of information and in discussing the thinking process one really has to go back to the situation itself since the choice of words in a description is already a choice of viewpoint, is already quite far along the thinking process. The nearest one can get to a raw situation, before it has been processed at all by thinking, is a visual situation and geometric ones are preferable since they are more definite and the processing of them is more easily studied. With verbal descriptions quite apart from the choice of viewpoint and the choice of words there are nuances of meaning which can lead to misunderstanding. With a visual situation no meaning is offered. The situation is just there and hence the same for everyone even though they may process it differently.

When the principles indicated by the artificial demonstrations have been understood, when there has been sufficient practice in the processes suggested, then one can move on to more real situations. It is exactly the same as learning mathematics on trivial and artificial problems and then using the processes on important ones.

The amount of material supplied in this book is very limited. What is supplied is supplied more as an example than as anything else. Anyone who is teaching lateral thinking, either to students or to his own children must supplement the material offered here with his own material.

● Visual material

The following material may be collected and used:

1. In the section dealing with the progressive arrangement of cardboard shapes one can make up this sort of shape and also devise new patterns for illustrating the same thing. In addition one can ask the students themselves to devise new shapes.

2. Photographs and pictures can be taken from newspapers and from magazines. These are especially useful in the section on different ways of looking at and interpreting a situation. The captions would naturally be removed. For convenience the pictures could be mounted on cardboard. If a magazine contained several useful pictures then a number of copies could be bought and used as permanent material.

3. Drawings of scenes or people in action can be provided by the students themselves. A drawing provided by one student is objective material for everyone else. The complexity or accuracy of the drawing is not important, since what matters is the way it is looked at by the others.

4. In the sections which call for the execution of designs as

drawings these provide abundant material not only for the current set of students but for subsequent ones.

● Verbal material

This can include written, spoken or recorded material.
1. Written material can be obtained from newspapers or magazines.
2. Written material can be supplied by the teacher writing on a particular theme with a definite (even if simulated) point of view.
3. Written material can be supplied by the students who are asked to write a short piece on some particular theme.
4. Spoken material can be derived from radio programmes, from recordings of radio programmes and from deliberate recording of simulated speeches.
5. Spoken material can be obtained from the students themselves, one of whom may be asked to talk about a certain subject.

● Problem material

The problem format is a convenient one for encouraging deliberate thinking. It is very difficult to think of a problem just when one is required. There are different sorts of problem.
1. General world problems such as food shortage. These are obviously open ended problems.
2. More immediate problems such as traffic control in cities. These are problems with which the students may have come into direct contact.
3. Immediate problems. These concern the direct everyday interaction at school. If one does deal with personal problems it is probably best to deal with them in an abstracted way as if talking about third parties.
4. Design and innovation problems. These are requests to bring about a certain effect. They usually apply to concrete objects but they can also apply to organization or ideas (e.g. how would you organize a babysitting service or a supermarket?).
5. Closed problems. These are problems for which there is a

definite answer. There is a way of doing something and it is seen to work when it is found. Such problems may be practical ones (for instance how to hang a washing line) or artificial ones (how to make a hole in a postcard big enough to put your head through). Problems can be derived from many different sources:

1. A general glance at a newspaper will generate world or more immediate problems (e.g. strikes).

2. Problems may be suggested by everyday life (e.g. more efficient train services).

3. Problems may be suggested by the students. The teacher asks for problems and then stockpiles the suggestions.

4. Design problems may be generated by taking any item (car, table, desk) and asking how it might be done in a better way. More elaborate design problems can be generated by taking some task which has to be performed by hand and asking for a machine to do the same thing – or a device to make it easier. One could also just ask for a simpler way to do it.

5. Closed problems are rather difficult to find. They must have a definite answer which is difficult enough to make the problem interesting but quite obvious once it has been found. There are some classic problems which one may know or be told about. It is however a bad idea to go to a puzzle book since many of the problems involve quite ordinary mathematical tricks which have nothing to do with lateral thinking. One simple way of generating closed problems is to take some ordinary task and then restrict the starting conditions. For instance one may want to draw a circle without using a compass. Once the problem has been set in this way then one solves it for oneself before offering it to others.

● Themes

There are times when one just wants a subject for consideration. These are not actual problems nor are they expressions of a particular point of view. It is a matter of having a subject area in which to move and develop ideas (e.g. cups, blackboard, books, acceleration, freedom, building). These can be obtained in various ways.

1. Simply by looking around one, taking an object and elaborating it into a theme.

2. By glancing at a newspaper and deriving a theme for each headline.

3. By asking the students to generate themes.

● Anecdotes and stories

These are probably the most effective way of putting across the lateral thinking idea but they are extremely difficult to generate.

1. From collections of fables or folk stories (e.g. Aesop's fables, the exploits of the Mulla Nasruddin).

2. By making a note of incidents from one's own experience or that of others, news items etc.

● Stockpile of material

It always seems much easier to think up material as required than it really is. It is better to gradually build up a stockpile of material: newspaper cuttings, photos, problems, stories, anecdotes, themes and ideas suggested by the students. One gradually builds up a file of such things and then can use them as needed. In addition there is the advantage that with use one can learn which items are particularly effective. One can also come to predict the standard responses to the items. Anecdotes, stories and problems should make a point about lateral thinking. Themes should be neutral, specific enough to excite definite ideas but wide enough for a variety of ideas to be offered. Pictures should be capable of different interpretations: a man holding a tin of corned beef is suitable but firemen putting out a fire are not; a woman looking in a mirror can be ambiguous, so can policemen arresting a man or soldiers marching down a street. It is enough if you yourself can think of at least two different interpretations.

In contrast the verbal material should be as definite as possible. An article should offer a committed point of view, even a fanatical point of view. A general uncommitted appraisal is not so much use unless one is looking for background information to help consideration of a theme.

In putting across the idea of lateral thinking, as in teaching any sort of thinking, it is possible to talk in abstract terms, but what really makes things clear is *actual involvement*. The involvement may start with abstract geometric shapes and then the process is transferred bodily to more real situations. It is useful to keep going back to the simple shapes to emphasize the process for if one sticks entirely to real situations the nature of the process may get very blurred. There is also the real danger that in considering real situations one comes to think in terms of collecting more information, whereas the whole idea of lateral thinking is concept restructuring.

Distinctness of lateral thinking

It may seem artificial to separate lateral thinking and try to teach it on its own when it is so much a part of thinking. There is a reason for doing this. Many of the processes of lateral thinking are quite contradictory to the other processes of thinking (it is their function to be so). Unless a clear distinction is made there is the danger of giving the impression that lateral thinking undermines what is being taught elsewhere by introducing doubt. It is by keeping lateral thinking distinct from vertical thinking that one can avoid this danger and come to appreciate the value of both. Lateral thinking is not an attack on vertical thinking, but a method of making it more effective by adding creativity.

The other danger which arises from failure to keep lateral thinking separate is the vague feeling that one is teaching it anyway in the course of teaching other things and therefore there is no need to do anything special about it. In practice such an attitude is quite wrong. Everyone naturally feels that they themselves use lateral thinking and that they always encourage it in their students. It is very easy to have this feeling but the fundamental nature of lateral thinking is so different from that of vertical thinking that it is impossible to teach both at the same time. It is not enough to introduce a mild flavour of lateral thinking One wants to develop enough skill in it for it to be used effectively, not just acknowledged as a possibility.

Organization of chapters of this book

Each chapter is divided into two parts:

1. Background material, theory and nature of the process being discussed in that section.

2. Practical format for trying out and using the process under discussion.

The need for lateral thinking arises from the way the mind works.* Though the information handling system called mind is highly effective it has certain characteristic limitations. These limitations are inseparable from the advantages of the system since both arise directly from the nature of the system. It would be impossible to have the advantages without the disadvantages. Lateral thinking is an attempt to compensate for these disadvantages while one still enjoys the advantages.

Code communication

Communication is the transfer of information. If you want someone to do something you could give him detailed instructions telling him exactly what to do. This would be accurate but it might take rather a long time. It would be much easier if you could simply say to him: 'Go ahead and carry out plan number 4.' This simple sentence might replace pages of instruction. In the

*A full account of how the mind handles information is given in the book, *The Mechanism of Mind*, published in Great Britain by Jonathan Cape (London, 1969), and by Pelican Books (Harmondsworth, 1971) and in the United States by Simon & Schuster (New York, 1969). It is obviously not possible to cover this matter in detail here for the purpose of this book is different. It is only possible to hint at the type of system involved. Wherever an asterisk occurs in the text (e.g. elsewhere*) those readers who require more detailed information are referred to the other book.

military world certain complex patterns of behaviour are coded in this manner so that one only has to specify the code number for the whole pattern of behaviour to be activated. It is the same with computers: much used programmes are stored under a particular heading and one can call them into use by just specifying that heading. When you go into a library to get a book you could describe in detail the book you wanted, giving author, title, subject, general outline etc. Instead of all that you could just give the code number from the catalogue.

Communication by code can only work if there are preset patterns. These patterns which may be very complex are worked out beforehand and are available under some code heading. Instead of transferring all the required information you just transfer the code heading. That code heading acts as a trigger word which identifies and calls up the pattern you want. This trigger word can be an actual code heading such as the name of a film or it can be some part of the information which acts to call up the rest. For instance one might not remember a film by its name but if one were to say: 'Do you remember that film with Julie Andrews as a governess looking after some children in Austria?' the rest of the film might be easily brought to mind.

Language itself is the most obvious code system with the words themselves as triggers. There are great advantages in any code system. It is easy to transfer a lot of information very quickly and without much effort. It makes it possible to react appropriately to a situation as soon as the situation is recognized from its code number without having to examine it in detail. It makes it possible to react appropriately to a situation before the situation has even developed fully – by identifying the situation from the initial aspects of it.

It is usual to think of communication as a two way affair: there is someone intending to send a message and someone trying to understand it. An arrangement of flags on a ship's mast is put there intentionally and anyone who understands the code can tell what it means. But a person who knows the code would also be able to pick out a message from a casual arrangement of flags used to decorate a party or a petrol station.

*

Communication can be a one way business. Dealing with the environment is an example of one way communication. One picks out messages from the environment even though no one has deliberately put them there.

If you offer a random arrangement of lines to a group of people they will soon start to pick out significant patterns. They will be convinced that the patterns have been put there deliberately or that the random arrangements are not random at all but actually constructed out of special patterns. Students who were asked to react in a certain way to a bell which was set off at random intervals soon became convinced that there was a meaningful pattern in the way the bell was sounded.

Communication by code or preset patterns requires the building up of a catalogue of patterns just as you can only use the catalogue number of a book in the library if someone has catalogued the books. As suggested above there does not have to be an actual code number for each pattern. Some part of the pattern itself may come to represent the whole pattern. If you recognized a man by hearing the name 'John Smith' that would be using a code heading, but if you recognized him by the sound of his voice at a party that would be using part of the pattern. Below are shown two familiar patterns, each of which is partly hidden behind some screen. One would have little difficulty in guessing the patterns from the parts that were accessible.

The mind as a pattern-making system

The mind is a pattern-making system. The information system of the mind acts to create patterns and to recognize them. This behaviour depends on the functional arrangement of the nerve cells of the brain.

The effectiveness of the mind in its one way communication with the environment arises from this ability to create patterns, store them and recognize them. It is possible that a few patterns are built into the mind and these become manifest as instinctual behaviour but this seems relatively unimportant in man as compared to lower animals. The mind can also accept ready made patterns that are fed to it. But the most important property of the system is the ability to create its own patterns. The way the mind actually creates patterns is described elsewhere.*

A system that can create its own patterns and recognize them is capable of efficient communication with the environment. It does not matter whether the patterns are right or wrong so long as they are definite. Since the patterns are always artificial ones created by the mind, it could be said that the function of mind is mistake. Once the patterns have been formed the selecting mechanism of usefulness (fear, hunger, thirst, sex, etc.) will sort out the patterns and keep those which are useful for survival. But first the patterns have to be formed. The selecting mechanism can only select patterns; it cannot form them or even alter them.

Self-organizing system

One can think of a secretary actively operating a filing system, of a librarian actively cataloguing books, of a computer actively sorting out information. The mind however does not actively sort out information. The information sorts itself out and organizes itself into patterns. The mind is passive. The mind only provides an opportunity for the information to behave in this way. The mind provides a special environment in which information can become self-organizing. This special environment is a memory surface with special characteristics.

A memory is anything that happens and does not completely unhappen. The result is some trace which is left. The trace may last for a long time or it may only last for a short time. Informa-

tion that comes into the brain leaves a trace in the altered behaviour of the nerve cells that form the memory surface.

A landscape is a memory surface. The contours of the surface
offer an accumulated memory trace of the water that has fallen
upon it. The rainfall forms little rivulets which combine into
streams and then into rivers. Once the pattern of drainage has
been formed then it tends to become ever more permanent since
the rain is collected into the drainage channels and tends to make
them deeper. It is the rainfall that is doing the sculpting and yet
it is the response of the surface to the rainfall that is organizing
how the rainfall will do its sculpting.

With a landscape the physical properties of the surface will
have a strong effect on the way the rainfall affects the surface.
The nature of the surface will determine what sort of river is
formed. Outcrops of rock will determine which way the river goes.

Instead of a landscape consider a homogeneous surface onto
which the rain falls. A shallow dish of table jelly would provide
such a surface. If hot water falls on this jelly surface it dissolves
a little bit of the jelly and when the water is poured off a shallow
depression is left in the surface. If another spoonful of water is
poured onto the surface near the first spoonful it will run into the
first depression tending to make this deeper but also leaving some
impression of its own. If successive spoonfuls of hot water are
poured onto the surface (pouring each one off again as soon as it
has cooled) the surface will become sculpted into a jelly landscape
of hollows and ridges. The homogeneous jelly has simply provided
a memory surface for the spoonfuls of hot water to organize themselves into a pattern. The contours of the surface are formed by
the water but once formed the contours direct where the water
will flow. The eventual pattern depends on *where the spoonfuls
of water were placed and in what sequence they were placed*.
This is equivalent to the nature of the incoming information and
the sequence of arrival. The jelly provides an environment for
the self-organization of information into patterns.

Limited attention span

A fundamental feature of a passive self-organizing memory system is the limited attention span. This is why only one spoonful of water at a time was poured onto the jelly surface. The mechanics of how a passive memory surface can come to have a limited attention span are explained elsewhere.* The limited attention span means that only part of the memory surface can be activated at any one time. Which part of the surface comes to be activated depends on what is being presented to the surface at the moment, what has been presented to the surface just before, and the state of the surface (i.e. what has happened to the surface in the past).

This limited attention span is extremely important for it means that the activated area will be a single coherent area and this single coherent area will be found in the most easily activated part of the memory surface. (In the jelly model this would mean the deepest hollow.) The most easily activated area or pattern is the most familiar one, the one which has been encountered most often, the one which has left most trace on the memory surface. And because a familiar pattern tends to be used it becomes ever more familiar. In this way the mind builds up that stock of preset patterns which are the basis of code communication.

With the limited attention span the passive self-organizing memory surface also becomes a self-maximizing one. This means that the processes of selection, rejection, combination and separation all become possible. Together these processes give the mind a very powerful computing function.*

Sequence of arrival of information

Opposite are shown the outlines of two pieces of thin plastic which are given to someone who is then instructed to arrange them together to give a shape that would be easy to describe. The two pieces are usually arranged to give a square as shown. Then another piece of plastic is added with the same instructions as before. This is simply added to the square to give a rectangle. Two more pieces are now added together. They are put together to give a slab which is added to the rectangle to give a square again. Finally another piece is added. But this new piece will not fit. Although one has been correct at each stage one is unable to proceed further. The new piece cannot be fitted into the existing pattern.

?

A different way of arranging the plastic pieces is shown below. With this new way of arranging them one can fit in all the pieces including the final one. Yet this other method is less likely to be tried than the first method since a square is so much more obvious than a parallelogram.

If one started off with the square then one would have to go back and *rearrange* the pieces at some stage to give a parallelogram before one could proceed. *Thus even though one had been correct at each stage one would still have to restructure the situation before being able to proceed.*

The plastic pieces indicate what happens in a self-maximizing system. In such a system information available at any moment is always arranged in the best way (most stable in physiological terms). As more information comes in it is added to the existing arrangement as the plastic pieces were added. But being able to make sense of the information at several stages does not mean that one can go on. There comes a time when one cannot proceed further without restructuring the pattern – without breaking up the old pattern which has been so useful and arranging the old information in a new way.

The trouble with a self-maximizing system that must make sense at each moment is that the sequence of arrival of information determines the way it is to be arranged. For this reason the *arrangement of information is always less than the best possible arrangement* for the best possible arrangement would be quite independent of the sequence of arrival of the pieces of information.

maximum use of
available information

Insight restructuring

ordinary use of
available information

In the mind which is a cumulative memory system the arrangement of information as concepts and ideas tends to make less than the maximum use of the information available. This is shown diagrammatically where the usual level of information use is shown well below the theoretical maximum level. It is by insight restructuring that one can move towards the maximal level.

Humour and insight

As with the plastic pieces there is often an alternative way of arranging available information. This means that there can be a switch over to another arrangement. Usually this switch over is sudden.* If the switch over is temporary it gives rise to humour. If the switch over is permanent it gives rise to insight. It is interesting that the reaction to an insight solution is often laughter even when there is nothing funny about the solution itself.

A man jumped off the top of a skyscraper. As he passed the third floor window he was heard to mutter: 'So far so good.'

Mr Churchill sat down next to Lady Astor at dinner one day. She turned to him and said, 'Mr Churchill, if I was married to you I should put poison in your coffee.' Mr Churchill turned to her and said, 'Madam, if I was married to you ... I should drink the coffee.'

A policeman was seen walking along the main street pulling a piece of string. Do you know why he was pulling the piece of string? ... Have you ever tried *pushing* a piece of string?

In each of these situations an expectation is generated by the way the information is put together. Then suddenly this expectation is thwarted but at once one sees that the unexpected development is another way of putting things together.

Humour and insight are characteristic of this type of information handling system. Both processes are difficult to bring about deliberately.

Disadvantages of the system

The advantages of the preset pattern information system have been mentioned. Basically the advantages are quickness of recognition and hence quickness of reaction. Because one can recognize what one is looking for one can also explore the environment efficiently. The disadvantages are just as definite. Some of the disadvantages of the information handling system of mind are listed here.

1. The patterns tend to become established ever more rigidly since they control attention.

2. It is extremely difficult to change patterns once they have become established.

3. Information that is arranged as part of one pattern cannot easily be used as part of a completely different pattern.

4. There is a tendency towards 'centering' which means that anything which has any resemblance to a standard pattern will be perceived as the standard pattern.

5. Patterns can be created by divisions which are more or less arbitrary. What is continuous may be divided into distinct units which then grow further apart. Once such units are formed they become self-perpetuating. The division may continue long after it has ceased to be useful or the division may intrude into areas where it has no usefulness.

In the diagram below on the left, if a square is habitually divided into quarters as shown in A it becomes difficult to use the division shown in B.

6. There is great continuity in the system. A slight divergence at one point can make a huge difference later.

7. The sequence of arrival of information plays too important a part in its arrangement. Any arrangement of information is thus unlikely to be the best possible arrangement of the information that is available.

8. There is a tendency to snap from one pattern to another instead of having a smooth change over. This is like those ink bottles which have two stable positions (see page 35 on the right). This snapping change occurs as one switches from one stable pattern to another.

9. Even though the choice between two competing patterns may be very fine one of them will be chosen and the other one completely ignored.

10. There is a marked tendency to 'polarize'. This means moving to either extreme instead of maintaining some balanced point between them.

11. Established patterns get larger and larger. That is to say individual patterns are strung together to give a longer and longer sequence which is so dominant that it constitutes a pattern on its own. There is nothing in the system which tends to break up such long sequences.

12. The mind is a cliché making and cliché using system.

The purpose of lateral thinking is to overcome these limitations by providing a means for restructuring, for escaping from cliché patterns, for putting information together in new ways to give new ideas. In order to do this lateral thinking makes use of the properties of this type of system. For instance the use of random stimulation could only work in a self-maximizing system. Also disruption and provocation are only of use if the information is then snapped together again to give a new pattern.

Summary

The mind handles information in a characteristic way. This way is very effective and it has huge practical advantages. But it also has limitations. In particular the mind is good at establishing concept patterns but not at restructuring them to bring them up to date. It is from these inherent limitations that the need for lateral thinking arises.

Since most people believe that traditional vertical thinking is the only possible form of effective thinking, it is useful to indicate the nature of lateral thinking by showing how it differs from vertical thinking. Some of the most outstanding points of difference are indicated below. So used are we to the habits of vertical thinking that some of these points of difference may seem sacrilegious. It may also seem that in some cases there is contradiction for the sake of contradiction. And yet in the context of the behaviour of a self-maximizing memory system lateral thinking not only makes good sense but is also necessary.

Vertical thinking is selective, lateral thinking is generative

Rightness is what matters in vertical thinking. Richness is what matters in lateral thinking. Vertical thinking selects a pathway by excluding other pathways. Lateral thinking does not select but seeks to open up other pathways. With vertical thinking one selects the most promising approach to a problem, the best way of looking at a situation. With lateral thinking one generates as many alternative approaches as one can. With vertical thinking one may look for different approaches until one finds a promising one. With lateral thinking one goes on generating as many approaches as one can even *after* one has found a promising one. With vertical thinking one is trying to select the best approach but with lateral thinking one is generating different approaches for the sake of generating them.

Vertical thinking moves only if there is a direction in which to move, lateral thinking moves in order to generate a direction

With vertical thinking one moves in a clearly defined direction towards the solution of a problem. One uses some definite approach or some definite technique. With lateral thinking one moves for the sake of moving.

One does not have to be moving towards something, one may be moving away from something. It is the movement or change that matters. With lateral thinking one does not move in order to follow a direction but in order to generate one. With vertical thinking one designs an experiment to show some effect. With lateral thinking one designs an experiment in order to provide an opportunity to change one's ideas. With vertical thinking one must always be moving usefully in some direction. With lateral thinking one may play around without any purpose or direction. One may play around with experiments, with models, with notation, with ideas.

The movement and change of lateral thinking is not an end in itself but a way of bringing about repatterning. Once there is movement and change then the maximizing properties of the mind will see to it that something useful happens. The vertical thinker says: 'I know what I am looking for.' The lateral thinker says: 'I am looking but I won't know what I am looking for until I have found it.'

Vertical thinking is analytical, lateral thinking is provocative

One may consider three different attitudes to the remark of a student who had come to the conclusion: 'Ulysses was a hypocrite.'

1. 'You are wrong, Ulysses was not a hypocrite.'
2. 'How very interesting, tell me how you reached that conclusion.'
3. 'Very well. What happens next? How are you going to go forward from that idea?'

In order to be able to use the provocative qualities of lateral thinking one must also be able to follow up with the selective qualities of vertical thinking.

Vertical thinking is sequential, lateral thinking can make jumps

With vertical thinking one moves forward one step at a time. Each step arises directly from the preceding step to which it is firmly connected. Once one has reached a conclusion the soundness of that conclusion is proved by the soundness of the steps by which it has been reached.

With lateral thinking the steps do not have to be sequential. One may jump ahead to a new point and then fill in the gap afterwards. In the diagram below, vertical thinking proceeds

steadily from A to B to C to D. With lateral thinking one may reach D via G and then having got there may work back to A.

When one jumps right to the solution then the soundness of that solution obviously cannot depend on the soundness of the path by which it was reached. Nevertheless the solution may still make sense in its own right without having to depend on the pathway by which it was reached. As with trial-and-error a successful trial is still successful even if there was no good reason for trying it. It may also happen that once one has reached a particular point it becomes possible to construct a sound logical pathway back to the starting point. Once such a pathway has been constructed then it cannot possibly matter from which end it was constructed – and yet it may only have been possible to construct it from the wrong end. It may be necessary to be on the top of a mountain in order to find the best way up.

With vertical thinking one has to be correct at every step, with lateral thinking one does not have to be

The very essence of vertical thinking is that one must be right at each step. This is absolutely fundamental to the nature of vertical thinking. Logical thinking and mathematics would not function at all without this necessity. In lateral thinking however one does not have to be right at each step provided the conclusion is right. It is like building a bridge. The parts do not have to be self-supporting at every stage but when the last part is fitted into place the bridge suddenly becomes self-supporting.

With vertical thinking one uses the negative in order to block off certain pathways. With lateral thinking there is no negative

There are times when it may be necessary to be wrong in order to be right at the end. This can happen when one is judged wrong according to the current frame of reference and then is found to be right when the frame of reference itself gets changed. Even if the frame of reference is not changed it may still be useful to go through a wrong area in order to reach a position from which the right pathway can be seen. This is shown diagrammatically below. The final pathway cannot of course pass through the wrong area but having gone through this area one may more easily discover the correct pathway.

wrong area

With vertical thinking one concentrates and excludes what is irrelevant, with lateral thinking one welcomes chance intrusions

Vertical thinking is selection by exclusion. One works within a frame of reference and throws out what is not relevant. With lateral thinking one realizes that a pattern cannot be restructured from within itself but only as the result of some outside influence. So one welcomes outside influences for their provocative action. The more irrelevant such influences are the more chance there is of altering the established pattern. To look only for things that are relevant means perpetuating the current pattern.

With vertical thinking categories, classifications and labels are fixed, with lateral thinking they are not

With vertical thinking categories, classifications and labels are useful only if they are consistent, for vertical thinking depends on identifying something as a member of some class or excluding it from that class. If something is given a label or put into a class it is supposed to stay there. With lateral thinking labels may change as something is looked at now in one way and now in another. Classifications and categories are not fixed pigeonholes to aid identification but signposts to help movement. With lateral thinking the labels are not permanently attached but are used for temporary convenience.

Vertical thinking depends heavily on the rigidity of definitions just as mathematics does on the unalterable meaning of a symbol

once this has been allocated. Just as a sudden change of meaning is the basis of humour so an equal fluidity of meaning is useful for the stimulation of lateral thinking.

Vertical thinking follows the most likely paths, lateral thinking explores the least likely

Lateral thinking can be deliberately perverse. With lateral thinking one tries to look at the least obvious approaches rather than the most likely ones. It is the willingness to explore the least likely pathways that is important for often there can be no other reason for exploring such pathways. At the entrance to an unlikely pathway there is nothing to indicate that it is worth exploring and yet it may lead to something useful. With vertical thinking one moves ahead along the widest pathway which is pointing in the right direction.

Vertical thinking is a finite process, lateral thinking is a probabilistic one

With vertical thinking one expects to come up with an answer. If one uses a mathematical technique an answer is guaranteed. With lateral thinking there may not be any answer at all. Lateral thinking increases the chances for a restructuring of the patterns, for an insight solution. But this may not come about. Vertical thinking promises at least a minimum solution. Lateral thinking increases the chances of a maximum solution but makes no promises.

If there were some black balls in a bag and just one white ball the chances of picking out that white ball would be low. If you went on adding white balls to the bag your chances of picking out a white ball would increase all the time. Yet at no time could you be absolutely certain of picking out a white ball. Lateral thinking increases the chances of bringing about insight restructuring and the better one is at lateral thinking the better are the chances. Lateral thinking is as definite a procedure as putting more white balls into the bag but the outcome is still probabilistic. Yet the pay off from a new idea or an insight restructuring of an old idea can be so huge that it is worth trying lateral thinking for there is nothing to be lost. Where vertical thinking has come up against a blank wall one would have to use lateral thinking even if the chances of success were very low.

Summary

The differences between lateral and vertical thinking are very fundamental. The processes are quite distinct. It is not a matter of one process being more effective than the other for both are necessary. It is a matter of realizing the differences in order to be able to use both effectively.

With vertical thinking one uses information for its own sake in order to move forward to a solution.

With lateral thinking one uses information not for its own sake but provocatively in order to bring about repatterning.

Because it is so very different from vertical thinking many people feel uncomfortable about lateral thinking. They would rather feel that it is just part of vertical thinking or that it does not exist. Some of the more standard attitudes are shown below.

Although one appreciates the effectiveness of insight solutions and the value of new ideas there is no practical way these can be brought about. One can only wait for them and recognize them after they have happened

This is a negative attitude which neither takes account of the insight mechanism nor of the information imprisoned in cliché patterns. Insight is brought about by alterations in pattern sequence brought about by provocative stimulation* and lateral thinking provides such stimulation. Information imprisoned in old cliché patterns can often come together in a new way of its own accord once the pattern is disrupted. It is a function of lateral thinking to free information by challenging cliché patterns. To regard insight and innovation as a matter of chance does not explain why some people are consistently able to generate more ideas than others. In any case one can take steps to encourage a chance process. The effectiveness of lateral thinking for generating new ideas can be shown experimentally.

Whenever a solution is said to have been reached by lateral thinking there is always a logical pathway by which the solution could have been reached. Hence what is supposed to be lateral thinking is no more than a plea for better logical thinking

It is quite impossible to tell whether a particular solution was reached by a lateral or vertical process. Lateral thinking is a description of a process not of a result. Because a solution could have been reached by vertical thinking does not mean that it was not reached by lateral thinking.

If a solution is acceptable at all then by definition there must be a logical reason for accepting it. It is always possible to describe a logical pathway in hindsight *once a solution is spelled out*. But being able to reach that solution by means of this hindsight pathway is another matter. One can demonstrate this quite simply by offering certain problems which are difficult to solve and yet when solved the solution is obvious. In such cases it is impossible to suppose that what made the problem difficult was lack of the elementary logic required.

It is characteristic of insight solutions and new ideas that they should be obvious after they have been found. In itself this shows how insufficient logic is in practice, otherwise such simple solutions must have occurred much earlier. In absolute terms it is impossible to prove that a logical pathway could not have been taken if one can be shown in hindsight (except by reference to the mechanics of information handling in the mind). In practical terms however it is quite obvious that the hindsight demonstration of a logical pathway does not indicate that the solution would have been reached in this way.

Since all effective thinking is really logical thinking then lateral thinking is just a part of logical thinking

This objection may seem to be just a semantic quibble. Obviously it does not matter at all whether lateral thinking is regarded as distinct from logical thinking or as part of logical thinking so long as one understands its true nature. If by logical thinking one just means effective thinking then lateral thinking must obviously be included. If by logical thinking one means a sequence of steps ~ach of which must be correct then lateral thinking is clearly distinct.

If the objection takes into account the information handling behaviour of the mind then it becomes more than a semantic quibble. For in terms of this behaviour it is logical to be illogical. It is reasonable to be unreasonable. If this was not so then I would not be writing a book about it. Here again however one is using logical in terms of 'effective' and not as the operational process we know.

In practice the inclusion of lateral thinking under logical thinking only blurs the distinction and tends to make it unusable – but not unnecessary.

Lateral thinking is the same as inductive logic

This argument is based on the distinction between deductive and inductive logic. The assumption is that anything which is different from deductive logic must be the same as anything else which is also different from deductive logic. There is some resemblance between inductive logic and lateral thinking in that both work from outside the framework instead of from within it. Even so lateral thinking can work from within the framework in order to bring about repatterning by such processes as reversal, distortion, query, turning upside down etc. Inductive logic is essentially reasonable: one tries just as hard to be right as in deductive logic. Lateral thinking however can be deliberately and self-consciously unreasonable in order to provoke a new pattern. Both inductive and deductive logic are concerned with concept forming. Lateral thinking is more concerned with concept breaking, with provocation and disruption in order to allow the mind to restructure patterns.

Lateral thinking is not a deliberate way of thinking at all but a creative gift which some people have and others do not

Some people may be better at lateral thinking just as some people may be better at mathematics but this does not mean that there is not a process which can be learned and used. It can be shown that lateral thinking can make people generate more ideas and by definition gifts cannot be taught. There is nothing mysterious about lateral thinking. It is a way of handling information.

Lateral thinking and vertical thinking are complementary

Some people are unhappy about lateral thinking because they feel that it threatens the validity of vertical thinking. This is not so at all. The two processes are complementary not antagonistic. Lateral thinking is useful for generating ideas and approaches and vertical thinking is useful for developing them. Lateral thinking enhances the effectiveness of vertical thinking by offering it more to select from. Vertical thinking multiplies the effectiveness of lateral thinking by making good use of the ideas generated.

Most of the time one might be using vertical thinking but when one needs to use lateral thinking then no amount of excellence in vertical thinking will do instead. To persist with vertical thinking when one should be using lateral thinking is dangerous. One needs some skill in both types of thinking.

Lateral thinking is like the reverse gear in a car. One would never try to drive along in reverse gear the whole time. On the other hand one needs to have it and to know how to use it for manoeuvrability and to get out of a blind alley.

In Chapter Two the nature of lateral thinking was indicated by contrasting it with vertical thinking. In this chapter the basic nature of lateral thinking is indicated in its own right.

Lateral thinking is concerned with changing patterns

By pattern is meant the arrangement of information on the memory surface that is mind. A pattern is a repeatable sequence of neural activity. There is no need to define it any more rigidly. In practice a pattern is any repeatable concept, idea, thought, image. A pattern may also refer to a repeatable sequence in time of such concepts or ideas. A pattern may also refer to an arrangement of other patterns which together make up an approach to a problem, a point of view, a way of looking at things. There is no limit to the size of a pattern. The only requirements are that a pattern should be repeatable, recognizable, usable.

Lateral thinking is concerned with changing patterns. Instead of taking a pattern and then developing it as is done in vertical thinking, lateral thinking tries to restructure the pattern by putting things together in a different way. Because the sequence of arrival of information in a self-maximizing system has so powerful an influence on the way it is arranged some sort of restructuring of patterns is necessary in order to make the best use of the information imprisoned within them.

In a self-maximizing system with a memory the arrangement of information must always be less than the best possible arrangement

The rearrangement of information into another pattern is insight restructuring. The purpose of the rearrangement is to find a better and more effective pattern.

A particular way of looking at things may have developed gradually. An idea that was very useful at one time may no longer be so useful today and yet the current idea has developed directly from that old and outmoded idea. A pattern may develop in a particular way because it was derived from the combination of two other patterns but had all the information been available at one time the pattern would have been quite different. A pattern may persist because it is useful and adequate and yet a restructuring of the pattern could give rise to something very much better.

In the diagram overleaf two pieces come together to give a pattern. This pattern then combines with another similar pattern in a straightforward manner. Without the addition of any new pieces the pattern can suddenly be restructured to give a much better pattern. Had all four pieces been presented at once this final pattern is the one that would have resulted, but owing to the *sequence of arrival* of the pieces it was the other pattern that developed.

Lateral thinking is both an attitude and a method of using information

The lateral thinking attitude regards any particular way of looking at things as useful but not unique or absolute. That is to say one acknowledges the usefulness of a pattern but instead of regarding it as inevitable one regards it as only one way of putting things together. This attitude challenges the assumption that what is a convenient pattern at the moment is the only possible pattern. This attitude tempers the arrogance of rigidity and dogma. The lateral thinking attitude involves firstly a refusal to accept rigid patterns and secondly an attempt to put things together in different ways. With lateral thinking one is always trying to generate alternatives, to restructure patterns. It is not a matter of declaring the current pattern wrong or inadequate. *Lateral thinking is never a judgement.* One may be quite satisfied

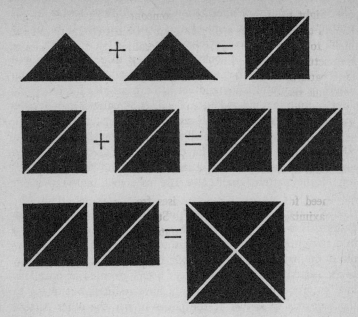

with the current pattern and yet try to generate alternative patterns. As far as lateral thinking is concerned the only thing that can be wrong with a pattern is the arrogant rigidity with which it is held.

In addition to being an attitude, lateral thinking is also a particular way of using information in order to bring about pattern restructuring. There are specific techniques which can be used deliberately and these will be discussed later. Underlying them all are certain general principles. In lateral thinking information is used not for its own sake but for its effect. This way of using information involves looking forward not backward: one is not interested in the reasons which lead up to and justify the use of a piece of information but in the effects that might follow such a use. In vertical thinking one assembles information into some structure, bridge or pathway. The information becomes part of the line of development. In lateral thinking information is used to alter the structure but not to become part of it.

One might use a pin to hold two pieces of paper together or

one might use a pin to jab into someone and make him jump. Lateral thinking is not stabilizing but provocative. It has to be in order to bring about repatterning. Because it is not possible to restructure a pattern by following the line of development of that pattern, lateral thinking may be deliberately perverse. For the same reason lateral thinking may use irrelevant information or it may involve suspending judgement and allowing an idea to develop instead of shutting it off by pronouncing it wrong.

Lateral thinking is directly related to the information handling behaviour of mind

The need for lateral thinking arises from the limitations of a self-maximizing memory system. Such a system functions to create patterns and then to perpetuate them. The system contains no adequate mechanism for changing patterns and bringing them up to date. Lateral thinking is an attempt to bring about this re-structuring or insight function.

Not only does the need for lateral thinking arise from the information handling of mind but the effectiveness of lateral thinking also depends on this behaviour. Lateral thinking uses information provocatively. Lateral thinking breaks down old patterns in order to liberate information. Lateral thinking stimulates new pattern formation by juxtaposing unlikely information. All these manoeuvres will only produce a useful effect in a self-maximizing memory system which snaps the information together again into a new pattern. Without this behaviour of the system lateral thinking would be purely disruptive and useless.

Once one has acquired the lateral thinking attitude one does not need to be told on what occasions to use lateral thinking.

Throughout this book lateral thinking is kept quite distinct from vertical thinking in order to avoid confusion. This is also done so that one can acquire some skill in lateral thinking without impairing one's skill in vertical thinking. When one is thoroughly familiar with lateral thinking one no longer has to keep it separate. One no longer has to be conscious whether one is using lateral or vertical thinking. The two blend together so that at one moment vertical thinking is being used and the next moment lateral thinking is being used. Nevertheless there are certain occasions which call for the deliberate use of lateral thinking.

New ideas

Most of the time one is not conscious of the need for new ideas even though one is grateful enough when they turn up. One does not try and generate new ideas because one suspects that new ideas cannot be generated by trying. Though new ideas are always useful there are times when one is very much aware of the need for a new idea. There are also jobs which demand a continual flow of new ideas (research, design, architecture, engineering, advertising etc).

The deliberate generation of new ideas is always difficult. Vertical thinking is not much help otherwise new ideas would be far easier to come by, indeed one would be able to programme a computer to churn them out. One can wait for chance or inspiration or one can pray for the gift of creativity. Lateral thinking is a rather more deliberate way of setting about it.

Many people suppose that new ideas mean new inventions in the form of mechanical contrivances. This is perhaps the most obvious form a new idea can take but new ideas include new ways of doing things, new ways of looking at things, new ways of organizing things, new ways of presenting things, new ideas about ideas. From advertising to engineering, from art to mathematics, from cooking to sport, new ideas are always in demand. This demand need not be just a general indication but can be as specific as one likes. One can actually set out to generate new ideas.

Problem solving

Even if one has no incentive to generate new ideas problems are thrust upon one. There is little choice but to try and solve them. A problem does not have to be presented in a formal manner nor is it a matter for pencil and paper working out. A *problem is simply the difference between what one has and what one wants.* It may be a matter of avoiding something, of getting something, of getting rid of something, of getting to know what one wants.

There are three types of problem:

● The first type of problem requires for its solution more information or better techniques for handling information.

● The second type of problem requires no new information but a rearrangement of information already available: an insight restructuring.

● The third type of problem is the problem of no problem. One is blocked by the adequacy of the present arrangement from moving to a much better one. There is no point at which one can focus one's efforts to reach the better arrangement because one is not even aware that there is a better arrangement. The problem is to realize that there is a problem – to realize that things can be improved and to define this realization as a problem.

The first type of problem can be solved by vertical thinking. The second and third type of problem require lateral thinking for their solution.

Processing perceptual choice

Logical thinking and mathematics are both second stage information processing techniques. They can only be used at the end of the first stage. In this first stage information is parcelled up by perceptual choice into the packages that are so efficiently handled by the second stage techniques. It is perceptual choice which determines what goes into each package. *Perceptual choice is the natural patterning behaviour of mind.* Instead of accepting the packages provided by perceptual choice and going ahead with logical or mathematical processing one might want to process the packages themselves. To do this one would have to use lateral thinking.

Periodic reassessment

Periodic reassessment means looking again at things which are taken for granted, things which seem beyond doubt. Periodic reassessment means challenging all assumptions. It is not a matter of reassessing something because there is a need to reassess it; there may be no need at all. It is a matter of reassessing something simply because it is there and has not been assessed for a long time. It is a deliberate *and quite unjustified* attempt to look at things in a new way.

Prevention of sharp divisions and polarizations

Perhaps the most necessary use of lateral thinking is when it is not used deliberately at all but acts as an attitude. As an attitude lateral thinking should prevent the emergence of those problems which are only created by those sharp divisions and polarizations which the mind imposes on what it studies. While acknowledging the usefulness of the patterns created by mind one uses lateral thinking to counter arrogance and rigidity.

The preceding chapters have dealt with the nature and use of lateral thinking. In reading through them one may have developed a clear idea of what lateral thinking is about. The more usual reaction is to understand and accept what has been written as one reads it and then to forget about it so quickly that one only retains a vague impression of what lateral thinking is about. Nor is this surprising because ideas are insubstantial things. Even if one did obtain a clear idea of the nature of lateral thinking it would be very difficult to pass on this idea without incorporating it in something more substantial.

A nodding acknowledgement of the purpose of lateral thinking is not much good. One has to develop some skill in the actual use of this type of thinking. Such skill can only develop if one has enough practice. Such practice ought not to await formal organization but it very often does. The techniques that are outlined in the following pages are meant to provide formal opportunities for practising lateral thinking. Some of the techniques may seem more lateral than others. Some of them may even seem to be things one always does anyway – or at least always imagines that one does.

Underlying each of these techniques are the basic principles of the lateral use of information. One does not have to stress these or lay them bare.

The purpose of the formal techniques is to provide an opportunity for the practical use of lateral thinking so that one may gradually acquire the lateral thinking habit. The techniques are not suggested as formal routines which must be exactly learned so that they can be deliberately applied thereafter. Nevertheless the techniques can be used in this manner and until one acquires sufficient fluency in lateral thinking to do without formal techniques one can use them as such.

Each section is divided into two parts. The first part is concerned with the nature and purpose of the technique. The second part consists of suggestions for the actual practice of the technique in a classroom or other setting. The material offered is only meant to suggest the sort of material that a teacher might assemble. The collection of further material and the handling of the practice sessions were discussed in the special section at the beginning of this book.

The most basic principle of lateral thinking is that any particular way of looking at things is only one from among many other possible ways. Lateral thinking is concerned with exploring these other ways by restructuring and rearranging the information that is available. The very word 'lateral' suggests the movement side-ways to generate alternative patterns instead of moving straight ahead with the development of one particular pattern. This is indicated in the diagrams below.

vertical

lateral

It may seem that the search for alternative ways of looking at something is a natural search. Many people feel that this is some-thing that they always do. To some extent it is, but the lateral search for alternatives goes far beyond the natural search.

In the natural search for alternatives one is looking for the best possible approach, in the lateral search for alternatives one is trying to produce as many alternatives as possible. One is not looking for the *best* approach but for as many *different* approaches as possible.

In the natural search for alternatives one stops when one comes to a promising approach. In the lateral search for alternatives one acknowledges the promising approach and may return to it later but one goes on generating other alternatives.

In the natural search for alternatives one considers only reasonable alternatives. In the lateral search for alternatives these do not have to be reasonable.

The natural search for alternatives is more often an intention than a fact. The lateral search for alternatives is deliberate.

The main difference is the purpose behind the search for alternatives. The natural inclination is to search for alternatives in order to find the best one. In lateral thinking however the purpose of the search is to loosen up rigid patterns and to provoke new patterns. Several things may happen with this search for alternatives.

One may generate a number of alternatives and then return to the original most obvious one.

A generated alternative might prove a useful starting point.
A generated alternative might actually solve the problems without further effort.

A generated alternative might serve to rearrange things so that the problem is solved indirectly.

Even if the search for alternatives proves to be a waste of time in a particular case it helps develop the habit of looking for alternatives instead of blindly accepting the most obvious approach.

The search for alternatives in no way prevents one from using the most obvious approach. The search merely delays the use of the most probable approach. The search merely adds a list of alternatives to the most probable approach but detracts nothing from it. In fact the search adds to the value of the most probable approach. Instead of this approach being chosen because it seems the only one, it is chosen because it is obviously the best from among many other possibilities.

Quota

In order to change the search for alternatives from being a good intention to a practical routine one can set a quota. A quota is a fixed number of alternative ways of looking at a situation. The advantage of having a predetermined quota is that one goes on generating alternatives until one has filled the quota and this means that if a particularly promising alternative occurs early in the search one acknowledges it and moves on instead of being captured by it. A further advantage of the quota is that one has to make an effort to find or generate alternatives instead of simply awaiting the natural alternatives. One makes an effort to fill the quota even if the alternatives generated seem artificial or even ridiculous. Suitable quotas might be three, four or five alternatives.

Having a quota does not of course stop one generating even more alternatives but it does ensure that one generates at least the minimum.

Practice

Geometric figures

The advantage of visual figures is that the material is presented
in an unequivocal form. A student may look at the material and
make of it what he will but the material remains the same. This
is in contrast to verbal material where tone, emphasis, individual
shades of meaning all give the material an individual flavour
which is not available to everyone.

The advantage of geometric figures is that they are standard
patterns described by simple words. This means that one can
snap from one description to another without any difficulty in
describing how one is looking at the figure.

figure

A
a triangle sitting
on a rectangle

B
a square with
two upper
corners missing

C
two halves of
a rectangle
put side by side

D
end view of
a house

The teacher starts off with the geometric figures in order to
indicate what the generation of alternatives is all about. When
the idea is clear he can move on to less artificial situations.

In practice the teacher handles the situation as follows:

1. The figure is shown on the board to the whole class or else
given out to each student on a separate piece of paper.

2. The students are asked to generate different ways of describing the figure.

3. The teacher can then collect the written alternatives or not, depending on the size of the classroom and the available time.

4a. (papers not collected)

The teacher asks for a volunteer description of the figure. If one is not forthcoming he points at someone and asks that person to describe the figure. Having got the first description the teacher asks for other variations. The other possible variations are listed.

4b. (papers collected)

The teacher may pick out one or two papers without needing to go through the lot. He reads out the description. He then asks for other variations or goes through the accumulated papers and picks out any variations.

If there is sufficient time between sessions the teacher could go through the papers and draw up a histogram list of the variations offered (as shown below). This is then shown at a subsequent session.

5. The function of the teacher is to encourage and accept variations, not to judge them. If a particular variation seems outrageous the teacher does not condemn it but asks the originator to explain it more fully. If it is obvious that the rest of the classroom cannot be persuaded to accept this outrageous variation then it is best to list it at the bottom. But it should not be rejected.

6. Whenever there is difficulty in generating variations the teacher must insert a few possibilities which he himself has prepared beforehand.

Material

1. How would you describe the figure shown below?

Alternatives

Two circles joined by a line.
A line with a circle at either end.
Two circles each with a short tail attached and placed so that the tails are in line and meet up.
Two pieces of guttering, one placed on top of the other.

Comment

It may be protested that 'two circles joined by a line' is really the same as a 'line with a circle at either end'. This is not so since in one case attention starts with the circle and in the other case it starts with the line. From the point of view of what happens in the mind the sequence of attention is of the utmost importance, hence a different sequence of attention is a difference.

Some of the descriptions may be static ones that can be explained in terms of the figure shown. Others may be dynamic descriptions which are more easily shown by additional diagrams.

This happens when the presented diagram is taken as the end point of some arrangement of other figures.

   2. How would you describe the figure shown below?

Alternatives

An L shape.
A carpenter's angle.
A gallows upside down.
Half a picture frame.
Two rectangles placed one against the other.
A large rectangle with a smaller rectangle subtracted.

Comment

Some difficulty arises when the presented shape is compared to an actual object like 'a carpenter's angle'. The difficulty is that this sort of description opens up an unlimited range of descriptions, for instance another description might describe the shape as a building looked at from the air. The point to keep very clearly in mind is that *one is asked for an alternative description of the presented figure, one is not asking what the figure could be or what it reminds you of.* The description must be such that someone could actually draw the figure from the description. Thus the suggestion that the figure looks like a building seen from the air is useless unless the building is specified as L-shaped in which case the description is L-shaped. One need not insist that the description be very exact, for instance the 'two rectangles placed one against the other' ought really to contain an indication of the orientation but one must not be pedantic because it misplaces the emphasis.

Some of the descriptions may indicate a particular process. Such descriptions as 'two rectangles placed one against the other' or 'a large rectangle with a smaller rectangle missing' actually require that one consider some other figure and then subtract or modify. Clearly this is a valid method of description. The basic types of description might be regarded as :

Building up from smaller units.

Comparing to another figure.

Modifying another figure by addition or subtraction.

As before one may have to draw additional diagrams to show what is meant. If one cannot understand oneself what the student means then he is asked to explain it himself.

3. How would you describe the figure shown below?

Alternatives

Two overlapping squares.

Three squares.

Two L shapes embracing a square gap.

A rectangle divided into half with the two pieces pushed out of line.

Comment

The 'two overlapping squares' seems so obvious a description that any other seems perverse. This illustrates how strong is the domination by obvious patterns. Once again it may be felt that 'two squares overlapping' is the same as 'three squares' since the latter is implied by the former. This is a tendency that must be resisted because often even a minor change in the way a thing is looked at can make a huge difference. One must resist the temptation to say that one description means the same thing as another and hence that it is just quibbling.

There may be elaborate descriptions which seek to be so comprehensive that they cover all possibilities: 'Two squares that overlap at one corner so that the area of overlap is a square of side about half that of the original squares'. Such comprehensive descriptions almost reproduce the diagram and hence must include all sorts of other descriptions. Nevertheless these other descriptions must be accepted in their own right. Logically a description may be redundant in that it is implied by another but perceptually the same description may make use of new patterns. For instance the idea of *three* squares is useful even though it is implicit in the overlap description.

4. How is the pattern opposite made up?

Alternatives

A small square surrounded by big squares.

A big square with small squares at the corners.

A column of large squares pushed sideways to give a staircase pattern.

Basic unit made out of one large and one small square.

Extend the edges of a small square and draw other small squares on these extended edges.

A line is divided into thirds and perpendiculars are drawn at each third.

In a grid pattern some of the small squares are designated in a certain way and outlined and then the lines are removed and the spaces filled with big squares.

Big squares are placed against each other so that the side of each one half overlaps the side of every adjacent square.

Two overlapped patterns of lines, one at right angles to the other.

Comment

There are very many possible variations other than those listed above. The descriptions offered must be workable. The description should clearly indicate how the pattern is being looked at. What is of importance is the variety of ways the pattern can be treated: in terms of large squares only, in terms of small squares only, in terms of both large and small squares, in terms of lines, in terms of spaces, in terms of a grid pattern.

● Activity

The examples used so far call for different descriptions of a presented pattern. One can move on from different ways of looking at things to different ways of doing things. This is rather more difficult since with description it is only a matter of selecting what is already there but to do something one has to put in what is not there.

5. How would you divide a square into four equal pieces? (For this example it is better that each student tries to draw as many different versions as he can instead of just watching the board and offering a new approach. At the end the papers may be collected if the teacher wants to analyse the results or else left with the students for them to tick off the various versions.)

Alternatives
Slices.
Four smaller squares.
Diagonals.
Divide the square into sixteen small squares and then put these together to give swastika or L shapes as shown overleaf.
Other shapes as shown overleaf.

Comment

Many students at first stick to the slices, diagonals and four small squares. One then introduces the idea of dividing the square into sixteen small squares and putting these together in different ways. The next principle is that any line which passes from a point on the edge of the square to an equivalent point on the opposite edge and has the same shape above the centre point as below it divides the square into half. By repeating the line at right angles one can divide the square into quarters. Obviously there is an infinite number of shapes which this line can have. It may be that some students will offer variations on this principle without realizing the principle. Rather than listing each variation one puts them together under the one principle. A variation on this principle involves dividing the square into half and then dividing each half into half again. For each half any division which passes

through the centre of that half and is of equivalent shape on each side of the centre point will do. This introduces a whole new range of shapes.

Since this is not an exercise in geometry or design the intention is not to explore the total possible ways of carrying out the division. What one tries to do is to show that there are other ways even when one is convinced that there cannot be. Thus the teacher waits until no further ways are offered and then introduces the variations suggested above, one at a time. (It may of course happen that all the variations listed above are introduced by the students themselves.)

6. How would you divide up a square of cardboard to give an L shape with the same area as the square? You can use not more than two cuts. (Actual squares of cardboard can be used or drawings should suffice.)

Alternatives

The two rectangular slices (see figure overleaf).
The cutting out of the small square.
The diagonal cut.

Comment

The requirement 'use not more than two cuts' introduces the element of constraint. The constraint is not meant to be restrictive, on the contrary it encourages the effort to find difficult alternatives instead of being easily satisfied.

Since one is used to dealing with vertical and horizontal lines and with right angles the diagonal method is not easy to find. Perhaps the best way to find it is to 'cut across the square diagonally and then see where that gets one'. In effect one is beginning to use provocative manoeuvres rather than simple analytical ones.

Non-geometrical shapes

Having used the geometrical shapes to illustrate the deliberate search for alternatives (and also the possibility of such alternatives) one can move on to more complex situations. In these more complex situations it is not so much a matter of picking out standard patterns as alternatives but of putting things together to give a pattern.

7. A one pint milk bottle with half a pint of water in it. How would you describe that bottle?

Alternatives
A half empty bottle of water.
A milk bottle half filled with water.
Half a pint of water in an empty one pint milk bottle.

Comment
In itself the milk bottle example is trivial. But it does serve to illustrate how there can be two completely different ways of looking at something. It also shows that when one way has been

chosen the alternative way is usually ignored. It is of interest that when the bottle is half filled with milk it is more often described as half empty, but when it is half filled with water it tends to be described as half full. This probably happens because in the case of the milk one is working downward from a full bottle but in the case of the water one is working upward from an empty milk bottle. The history of a situation has much effect on the way it is looked at.

● Pictures

Photographs from newspapers or magazines are the most easily available source of pictures. The difficulty is to make them available to a large group. This could be done by getting individual copies of a newspaper and keeping them until the material is out of date. If sufficiently skilled the teacher could actually draw pictures on the board but this is much less satisfactory. The type of material needed has been discussed in the section 'Use of this book'.

Pictures can be used in two ways :
● Describe what you think is happening in that picture.
● Describe three different things that could be happening in that picture.

In method 1 the teacher uses an ambiguous picture and asks each person to make his own interpretation. At the end he collects the interpretations. Variability between individual interpretations shows the alternative ways of looking at the picture. The teacher is careful not to judge which way is best or why one way is unreasonable. Nor does he reveal what the picture was actually about (he can conveniently have forgotten this).

In method 2 the students are asked to generate a quota of different interpretations. If the students tend to be blocked by the most obvious interpretation and are unwilling to guess at any others then they may be allowed to list the interpretations in order of likelihood. In addition the teacher throws in some outlandish suggestions about the particular picture being used in order to suggest what is required.

Examples

A photograph showing a group of people wading through shallow water. They are not dressed for paddling. In the background appears to be a beach. The following interpretations were received:

A group of people caught by the tide.
People crossing a flooded river.
People wading out to an island or sand spit.
Wading through flood water.
People wading out to a ferry boat which cannot come inshore.
People coming ashore from a wrecked boat.

Comment

In fact the photograph showed a group of people protesting at the poor state of the beach. It was not important that anyone should have guessed this since it was not an exercise in logical deduction. What was important was that there were several different interpretations of what was going on. Apart from noting these variations one should have been able to generate them (even if only to reject them).

Example

Photograph of a boy sitting on a park bench.

Alternatives

Picture of an inactive or lazy boy.
An empty space on a park bench.
Part of the bench is being kept dry by the boy.

Comment

The description of this picture is quite different from the other example. There is less attempt to say what is happening (e.g. a boy waiting for his pals, a tired boy resting, a boy playing truant from school, a boy enjoying the sun). Instead the description is directed at the scene itself rather than the meaning (e.g. a boy on a park bench, an empty space on the bench). There is also an attempt to look at the picture in an unusual way. This might have gone too far with 'part of the bench being kept dry by the boy' but there really are no limits. In any picture there are several different levels of description: what is shown, what is going on, what has happened, what is about to happen. In asking for alternatives the teacher may leave it quite open at first but later on he specifies the level of description within which the alternatives have to be generated.

● Altered pictures

The trouble with pictures is that too often the obvious interpretation is completely dominant. Not only is it difficult to find other ways of looking at it but these other ways seem silly and artificial. To avoid this difficulty and to make things more interesting the teacher can alter pictures by covering up parts of them. It immediately becomes far more difficult to tell what the picture is about from the exposed part and thus one is able to generate alternative possibilities without being dominated by an obvious interpretation. There is also the added incentive of trying to guess the right answer which will be obvious when the full picture is revealed.

Example

Half of a picture is obscured. What is revealed is a man balancing on the edge of a ledge running along the side of some building.

Alternatives

A man threatening to commit suicide.
Rescuing a cat that has got stuck on a ledge.
Escaping from a burning building.
Film stunt man.
A man trying to get into his room, having locked himself out.

Comment

The rest of the picture would have shown some student posters which the man was sticking up. The use of partial pictures makes it easier to generate alternatives but ultimately one wants to be able to restructure pictures in which an obvious interpretation makes it difficult to find alternative structurings. It is especially those situations which are dominated by an obvious interpretation that one wants to practise restructuring. One can use the easier partial pictures, however, to acquire experience. Another advantage of the partial picture is that it indicates that the interpretation may lie outside what is visible. This makes one inclined to look about not only at what is in the actual situation being examined but at things outside it.

● Written material – Stories

Stories may be obtained from newspapers or magazines or even from books that are being used elsewhere in the curriculum. By story is not meant a tale but any written account.

Stories may be treated in the following ways:

● Generate the different points of view of the people involved.

● Change what is a favourable description to an unfavourable one not by changing the material but by changing the emphasis and looking at it in a different way.

● Extract a different significance from the information given than that extracted by the writer.

Example

Newspaper story of an eagle that has escaped from the zoo and is proving difficult to capture. It is perched on a high branch and is resisting the efforts of the keepers to lure it back to its cage.

Alternatives

The keeper's point of view: the bird may fly away and get lost or shot unless it is coaxed back soon. It is uncomfortable having to climb up trees after the bird and one feels a bit of a fool. Someone is to blame for having let it escape.

The newspaperman's point of view: the longer the bird stays out the better the story. Can one get close enough to get a good pictures? One ought to find some other interest such as different people's ideas on how to catch the bird.

The eagle's point of view: wondering what all the fuss is about. Strange feeling not to be in a cage. Getting rather hungry. Not sure in which direction to fly.

The onlooker's point of view: hoping the eagle will fly away and be free for evermore. Amused to see the strenuous efforts being made to catch the bird. The eagle looks so much better out on its own than inside a cage. Perhaps one could show how clever one was by catching the bird when no one else could.

Comment

Whenever there is a story with different people involved then it is a simple matter to try to generate the point of view of everyone concerned. Every student could try to generate the different points of view or else different students could be assigned to generate the different points of view. The exercise is not so much to try to guess what other people are thinking but to show how the same situation can be structured in different ways.

Example

A story describing the uncomfortable life in a primitive community where the people cannot read or write and where only a bare subsistence can be obtained by hard work in the fields.

Alternatives

Comfort as a matter of what one was used to. If one was used to simple things and could obtain simple things perhaps this was better than expecting complex things and being dissatisfied when one could not obtain them.

Perhaps reading and writing only upset people by making them aware of the awful things that are happening in the rest of the world. Perhaps reading and writing make people more dissatisfied.

Most people are usually working hard at something or other; perhaps hard work in the field is more rewarding since one can actually see something growing and one is actually going to eat what one grows.

Comment

The alternative point of view does not necessarily have to be the point of view held by the person generating it. The person may actually hold exactly the same point of view as the writer. The purpose is to show that one can look at things in a different way.

Nor is it a matter of trying to prove one point of view to be better than the other. There is no question of arguing for instance 'that the simple community may seem pleasant but if one is ill one must just die etc.' In practice it is difficult to avoid arguing. It is also difficult to put forward a point of view with which one does not agree. The advantage of being able to put forward an opposing point of view is that one then has much more chance of restructuring it.

Example

A story may cite the long hair and colourful clothes of young men as an example that they were being demasculinized and becoming effeminate; that one could no longer distinguish between boys and girls.

Alternatives

Wearing long hair shows courage, it shows the courage to defy conventions.

Until quite recently men always wore long hair as in the Elizabethan era and far from being less masculine they were more masculine. As for the colourful clothes these were flamboyant not feminine. They indicated a masculine search for individuality.

In any case why shouldn't boys and girls look alike?

In that way at least girls would get equal rights.

Comment

In this type of restructuring no extra information may be introduced. It is definitely not meant to be a presentation of the other side of the case. The purpose is to show that the material put together to give one point of view can also be put together in a completely different way.

Problems

Problems can be generated from the inconveniences of everyday living or by looking through a newspaper. Newspaper columns are full of difficulties, disturbances, things that have gone wrong and complaints. Though these may not actually be stated as problems they can easily be rephrased as such. It is enough that a general problem theme be stated; there is no need to set up a formal problem. Any situation where there is room for improvement can be used as a problem and also any difficulty that can be imagined.

In using problem material to exercise the generation of alternatives one may proceed in two ways:

1. Generate alternative ways of stating the problem.
2. Generate alternative approaches to the problem.

The emphasis is not on actually trying to solve the problem but on finding different ways of looking at the problem situation. One may go on towards a solution but this is not essential.

Example

The problem of children getting separated from their parents in large crowds.

Alternatives

1. Restatements

Preventing separation of children from parents.
Preventing children being lost.
Finding or returning lost children.
Making it unnecessary for parents to have to take children into large crowds (crèches at exhibitions etc).

Comment

Some of the alternative statements of the problem do suggest answers. The more general the statement of a problem the less likely is it to suggest answers. If a problem is stated in very general terms then it is not easy to restate the problem in another way on the same level of generality. If this is the case one can always descend to a more specific level in order to generate alternatives. For instance 'the problem of lost children in crowds' could be restated as the 'problem of careless parents in crowds' or 'the problem of children in crowds' but one could also use a more specific level such as 'the problem of returning lost children to their parents'.

2. Different approaches

Alternatives

Attach children more firmly to their parents (by a dog's lead?).
Better identification of children (disc with address).
Make it unnecessary for children to be taken into the crowd (crèches etc).
Central points for children and parents to get to if losing sight of one another.
Display list of lost children.

Comment

In this case many of the approaches seem like actual solutions. In other situations however approaches may just indicate a way of tackling the problem. For instance with this lost children problem one approach might be 'Collect statistical data on how many people take their children into crowds because they want the children to be there or because there is no one the children can be left with.'

● Type of problem

The type of problem used depends very much on the age of the students involved. The problem suggestions listed below are divided into a young age group and an older one.

Young age group

Making washing up easier or quicker.
Getting to school on time.
Making bigger ice creams.
Getting a ball that is stuck in a tree.
How to manage change on buses.
Better umbrellas.

Older age group

Traffic jams.
Room for airports.
Making railways pay.
Enough low cost housing.

World food problem.
What should cricketers do in winter?
Better design for a tent.

Summary

This chapter has been concerned with the deliberate generation of alternatives. This generation of alternatives is for its own sake and not as a search for the best way of looking at things. The best way may become obvious in the course of the procedure but one is not actually trying to find out. If one were just looking for the best approach then one would stop as soon as one found what appeared to be the best approach. Instead of stopping however one goes on with the generation of alternatives for its own sake. The purpose of the procedure is to loosen up rigid ways of looking at things, to show that alternative ways are always present if one bothers to look for them, and to acquire the habit of restructuring patterns.

It is probably better to use the artificial quota method rather than just rely on the general intention for trying to find other ways of looking at things. General intentions work well when things are easy but not when they are difficult. The quota sets a limit which *must* be met.

The previous chapter was concerned with alternative ways of putting things together. It was a matter of finding out alternative ways of putting A, B, C and D together to give different patterns. This section is concerned with A, B, C and D for their own sakes. Each of them is itself an accepted, standard pattern.

A cliché is a stereotyped phrase, a stereotyped way of looking at something or describing something. But clichés refer not only to arrangements of ideas but to ideas themselves. It is usually assumed that the basic ideas are sound and then one starts fitting them together to give different patterns. But the basic ideas are themselves patterns that can be restructured. It is the purpose of lateral thinking to challenge any assumption for it is the purpose of lateral thinking to try and restructure any pattern. General agreement about an assumption is no guarantee that it is correct. *It is historical continuity that maintains most assumptions – not a repeated assessment of their validity.*

The figure opposite shows three shapes. Suppose you had to arrange them to give a single shape that would be easy to describe? There is difficulty in finding such an arrangement. But if, instead of trying to fit the given shapes together, one reexamined each shape then one might find it possible to split the larger square into two. After that it would be easy to arrange all the shapes into an overall simple shape. This analogy is only meant to illustrate how sometimes a problem cannot be solved by trying different arrangements of the given pieces but only by reexamination of the pieces themselves.

If the above problem was actually set as a problem and the solution given as indicated, there would immediately be an out-

cry that this was 'cheating'. There would be protests that it was
assumed that the given shapes could not themselves be altered.
Such a cry of 'cheating' always reveals the use of certain assumed
boundaries or limits.

In problem solving one always assumes certain boundaries.
Such boundaries make it much easier to solve the problem by
reducing the area within which the problem solving has to take
place. If someone were to give you an address in London it might
be hard to find. If someone told you it was north of the Thames
it would be slightly easier to find. If someone told you that it was
within walking distance of Piccadilly Circus it would be that
much easier to find. So it is with problem solving that one sets
one's own limits within which to explore. If someone else comes
along and solves the problem by stepping outside the limits there
is an immediate cry of 'cheating'. And yet the limits are usually
self-imposed. Moreover they are imposed on no stronger grounds
than that of convenience. If such boundaries or limits are wrongly

set then it may be as impossible to solve the problem as it would be to find an address south of the river Thames by looking north of the river.

Since it would be quite impossible to reexamine everything in sight one has to take most things for granted in any situation – whether or not it is a problem situation. Late one Saturday morning I was walking down a shopping street when I saw a flower seller holding out a large bunch of carnations for which he was only charging two shillings (ten new pence). It seemed a good bargain and I assumed that it was the end of the morning and he was getting rid of his leftover flowers. I paid him, whereupon he detached a small bunch of about four carnations from the large bunch and handed them to me. The little bunch was a genuine bunch wrapped with a little bit of wire. It was only my greed that had assumed that the bunch offered had referred to the whole bunch he held in his hand.

A new housing estate had just been completed. At the ceremonial opening it was noticed that everything appeared to be a little bit low. The ceilings were low, the doors were low, the windows were low. No one could understand what had happened. Finally it was discovered that someone had sabotaged the measuring sticks used by the workmen by cutting an inch off the end of each one. Naturally everyone using the sticks had assumed that they at least were correct since they were used to show the correctness of everything else.

There is made in Switzerland a pear brandy in which a whole pear is to be seen within the bottle. How did the pear get into the bottle? The usual guess is that the bottle neck has been closed after the pear has been put into the bottle. Others guess that the bottom of the bottle was added after the pear was inside. It is always assumed that since the pear is a fully grown pear that it must have been placed in the bottle as a fully grown pear. In fact if a branch bearing a tiny bud was inserted through the neck of the bottle then the pear would actually grow within the bottle and there would be no question of how it got inside.

In challenging assumptions one challenges the necessity of boundaries and limits and one challenges the validity of individual concepts. As in lateral thinking in general there is no question of attacking the assumptions as wrong. Nor is there any question of offering better alternatives. It is simply a matter of trying to restructure patterns. And by definition assumptions are patterns which usually escape the restructuring process.

Practice session

1. Demonstration problems

Problem

A landscape gardener is given instructions to plant four special trees so that each one is exactly the same distance from each of the others. How would you arrange the trees?

The usual procedure is to try and arrange four dots on a piece of paper so that each dot is equidistant from every other dot. This turns out to be impossible. The problem seems impossible to solve.

The assumption is that the trees are all planted on a level piece of ground. If one challenges this assumption one finds that the trees can indeed be planted in the manner specified. But one tree is planted at the top of a hill and the other three are planted on the sides of the hill. This makes them all equidistant from one another (in fact they are at the angles of a tetrahedron). One can also solve the problem by placing one tree at the bottom of a hole and the others around the edge of the hole.

Problem

This is an old problem but it makes the point very nicely. Nine dots are arranged as shown overleaf. The problem is to link up these nine dots using only four straight lines which must follow on without raising the pencil from the paper.

At first it seems easy and various attempts are made to link up the dots. Then it is found that one always needs more than four. The problem seems impossible.

The assumption here is that the straight lines must link up the dots and must not extend beyond the boundaries set by the outer line of dots. If one breaks through this assumption and does go beyond the boundary then the problem is easily solved as shown.

Problem

A man worked in a tall office building. Each morning he got in the lift on the ground floor, pressed the lift button to the tenth floor, got out of the lift and walked up to the fifteenth floor. At night he would get into the lift on the fifteenth floor and get out again on the ground floor. What was the man up to?

Various explanations are offered. They include:

The man wanted exercise.

He wanted to talk to someone on the way up from the tenth to the fifteenth floor.

He wanted to admire the view as he walked up.

He wanted people to think he worked on the tenth floor (it might have been more prestigious) etc.

In fact the man acted in this peculiar way because he had no choice. He was a dwarf and could not reach higher than the tenth floor button.

The natural assumption is that the man is perfectly normal and it is his behaviour that is abnormal.

One can generate other problems of this sort. One can also collect examples of behaviour which seem bizarre until one knows the real reason behind it. The purpose of these problems is just to show that the acceptance of assumptions may make it difficult or impossible to solve a problem.

2. The block problems

Problem

Take four blocks (these may be matchboxes, books, cereal or detergent packets). The problem is to arrange them in certain specified ways. These ways are specified by how the blocks come to touch each other in the arrangement. For two blocks to be regarded as touching, any part of any flat surface must be in contact – a corner or an edge does not count.

The specified arrangements are as follows:

1. Arrange the blocks so that each block is touching two others.

2. Arrange the blocks so that one block is touching one other, one block is touching two others, and another block is touching three others.

3. Arrange the blocks so that each block is touching three others.

4. Arrange the blocks so that each block is touching one other.

Solutions

1. There are several ways of doing this. One way is shown on p. 89. This is a 'circular' arrangement in which each block has

two touching neighbours – one in front and one behind.

2. There is often some difficulty with this one because it is *assumed* that the problem has to be solved in the sequence in which it was posed, i.e. one block to touch one other, one block to touch two others, one block to touch three others. If, however, a start is made at the other end by making one block touch three others then this arrangement can be progressively modified to give the arrangement shown.

3. Some people have a lot of difficulty with this problem because they *assume* that all the blocks have to lie in the same plane (i.e. spread out on the surface being used). As soon as one breaks free of this assumption and starts to place the blocks on top of one another one can reach the required arrangement.

4. There is a surprising amount of difficulty in solving this problem. The usual mistake is to arrange the blocks in a long row. In such a row the end blocks are indeed touching only one other but the middle blocks have two neighbours. A few people actually declare that the problem cannot be solved. The correct arrangement is very simple.

Comment

Most people solve the block arranging problems by playing around with the blocks and seeing what turns up. Nothing much would happen if one did this without bothering to have the blocks touching one another. So for convenience one assumes that the blocks all have to touch one another in some fashion (i.e. there has to be a single arrangement). It is this artificial limit, this assumption, that makes it so difficult to solve the last problem which is so easy in itself.

The 'Why' Technique

This is a game which provides an opportunity for practising the challenging of assumptions. It can also be used as a deliberate technique. The 'why' technique is very similar to the usual child's habit of asking 'why' all the time. The difference is that 'why' is

usually asked when one does not know the answer, whereas with the 'why' technique it is asked when one does know the answer. The usual response to 'why' is to explain something unfamiliar in terms that are familiar enough to be an acceptable explanation. With the 'why' technique these familiar terms are questions as well. Nothing is sacred.

The process is rather more difficult than it seems. There is a natural tendency to run out of explanations or to circle back and give an explanation that has already been used before. There is also the very natural tendency to say 'because' if something very obvious is questioned. The whole point of the exercise is to avoid feeling that anything is so obvious that it merits a 'because' answer.

The teacher makes some sort of statement and then a student asks, 'Why?' The teacher offers an explanation which is in turn met by another, 'Why?' If the process was no more than an automatic repetition of 'why' then one would hardly need a second party to ask 'why' except that the student gets into the habit of assuming nothing. In practice it never is an automatic repetition of 'why'. The question is directed to some particular aspect of the previous explanation rather than being a blanket response. 'Why' can be focused.

Examples

Why are blackboards black?
Because otherwise they would not be called blackboards.
Why would it matter what they were called?
It would not matter.
Why?
Because they are there to write or draw upon.
Why?
Because if something is to be shown to the whole classroom it is easier to write on the blackboard where everyone can see it.

The above questioning might however have taken quite a different line.
Why are blackboards black?
So that the white chalk marks can be seen easily.

Why do you want to see the white chalk marks?
or:
Why is the chalk white?
or:
Why does one want to use white chalk?
or:
Why don't you use black chalk?

In each of these cases 'why' is directed to a particular aspect of the subject and this determines the development of the questioning. The teacher can of course also direct the development by the way the question is answered.

The teacher keeps up the answers as long as possible. He may however at any time say: 'I don't know. Why do you think?' If the student can give an answer then the roles can be reversed with the student answering the why questions and the teacher putting them.

Some possible subjects for this type of session are given below:
Why are wheels round?
Why does a chair have four legs?
Why are most rooms square or oblong?
Why do girls wear different clothes from boys?
Why do we come to school?
Why do people have two legs?

The usual purpose of 'why' is to elicit information. One wants to be comforted with some explanation which one can accept and be satisfied with. The lateral use of why is quite opposite. The intention is to create discomfort with any explanation. By refusing to be comforted with an explanation one tries to look at things in a different way and so increases the possibility of re-structuring the pattern.

In answering the question the teacher does not have to struggle to justify something as a unique explanation. In his answer he can suggest alternatives. The answer to the question, 'Why does the blackboard have to be black?' could be, 'It does not have to be black, it could be green or blue so long as the white chalk showed.' The impression that there is a unique and necessary reason behind everything must be avoided. Contrast the answers:

'Blackboards are black because black is a convenient colour to show up white chalk marks.'

'Blackboards are black because otherwise you would not see what was written on them.'

Even if there is a true historic reason behind something the teacher must not give the impression that the historic reason is a sufficient one. Suppose that blackboards really were black because the usefulness of white chalk was discovered first. Historically this is an accurate reason for the use of black but in practice it is not enough. After all it only explains why people started to use black but does not explain why it is convenient to continue doing so. One might say: 'Blackboards were originally coloured black because they were looking for a surface to show up the white chalk marks. They have continued to be black ever since because black has proved satisfactory.'

Summary

In dealing with situations or problems many things have to be taken for granted. In order to live at all one must be making assumptions all the time. Yet each of these assumptions is a cliché pattern which may be restructured to make better use of available information. In addition the restructuring of more complex patterns may prove impossible unless one breaks through some assumed boundary. The idea is to show that any assumption whatsoever can be challenged. It is not a matter of pretending that one has time to challenge every assumption on every occasion but of showing that nothing is sacred.

The idea is not to sow so much doubt that one is reduced to dithering indecision through being unable to take anything for granted. On the contrary one acknowledges the great usefulness of assumptions and clichés. In fact one is much freer to use assumptions and clichés if one knows that one is not going to be imprisoned by them.

The two preceding chapters have been concerned with two fundamental aspects of the lateral thinking process:
● The deliberate generation of alternative ways of looking at things.
● The challenging of assumptions.

In themselves these processes are not far removed from ordinary vertical thinking. What is different is the 'unreasonable' way in which the processes are applied and the purpose behind the application. Lateral thinking is concerned not with development but with restructuring.

Both the processes mentioned above have been applied for the purpose of description or analysis of a situation. This could be called backward thinking: this is a matter of looking at something that is there and working it over. Forward thinking involves moving forward. Forward thinking involves building up something new rather than analysing something old. Innovation and creativity involve forward thinking. The distinction between backward and forward thinking is entirely arbitrary. There is no real distinction because one may have to look backward in a new way in order to move forward. A creative description may be just as generative as a creative idea. Both backward thinking and forward thinking are concerned with alteration, with improvement, with bringing about some effect. In practice backward thinking is however more concerned with explaining an effect whereas forward thinking is more concerned with bringing about an effect.

Before going on to consider innovation it is necessary to

consider an aspect of thinking that applies much more to forward thinking than to backward thinking. This is the matter of evaluation and suspended judgement.

The purpose of thinking is not to be right but to be effective. Being effective does eventually involve being right but there is a very important difference between the two. Being right means being right all the time. Being effective means being right only at the end.

Vertical thinking involves being right all along. Judgement is exercised at every stage. One is not allowed to take a step that is not right. One is not allowed to accept an arrangement of information that is not right. Vertical thinking is selection by exclusion. Judgement is the method of exclusion and the negative ('no', 'not') is the tool of exclusion.

With lateral thinking one is allowed to be wrong on the way even though one must be right in the end. With lateral thinking one is allowed to use arrangements of information which are invalid in themselves in order to bring about a restructuring that is valid. One may have to move to an untenable position in order to be able to find a tenable position.

In lateral thinking one is not so concerned with the nature of an arrangement of information but with where it can lead one. So instead of judging each arrangement and allowing only those that are valid one suspends judgement until later on. It is not a matter of doing without judgement but of deferring it until later.

As a process lateral thinking is concerned with change not with proof. The emphasis is shifted from the validity of a particular pattern to the usefulness of that pattern in generating new patterns.

There is nothing 'unreasonable' about the other lateral thinking processes described so far but the need to suspend judgement is so fundamentally different from vertical thinking that it is much harder to understand.

Education is soundly based on the *need to be right all the time*. Throughout education one is taught the correct facts, the correct deductions to be made from them and the correct way of making these deductions. One learns to be correct by being made very sensitive to what is incorrect. One learns to apply judgement at every stage and to follow up this judgement with the 'no' label. One learns how to say, 'no', 'this is not so', 'this cannot be so', 'this does not lead to that', 'you are wrong here', 'this would never work', 'there is no reason for that' and so on. This sort of thing is the very essence of vertical thinking and accounts for its great usefulness. The danger lies in the arrogance of the attitude that assumes that vertical thinking is sufficient. It is not. Exclusive emphasis on the need to be right all the time completely shuts out creativity and progress.

The need to be right all the time is the biggest bar there is to new ideas. It is better to have enough ideas for some of them to be wrong than to be always right by having no ideas at all.

The need to make use of provocative arrangements of information in order to bring about insight repatterning is dictated by the behaviour of mind as a self-maximizing memory system.* In practice this need is met by delaying judgement. Judgement is suspended during the generative stage of thinking in order to be applied during the selective stage. The nature of the system is such that a wrong idea at some stage can lead to a right one later on. Lee de Forest discovered the immensely useful thermionic valve through following up the erroneous idea that an electric spark altered the behaviour of a gas jet. Marconi succeeded in transmitting wireless waves across the Atlantic ocean through following up the erroneous idea that the waves would follow the curvature of the earth.

The major dangers of the need to be right all the time are as follows :

● Arrogant certainty attends a line of thought which though correct in itself may have started from wrong premises.

● An incorrect idea which would have led on to a correct idea (or useful experimentation) is choked off at too early a stage if it cannot itself be justified.

● It is assumed that being right is enough – an *adequate* arrangement blocks the possibility of a better arrangement.

● The importance attached to being right all the time breeds the inhibiting fear of making mistakes.

Delay in judgement

A later chapter deals with the lateral process which involves being wrong on purpose in order to provoke a rearrangement of information. What is being considered here is simply the *delaying of judgement* instead of applying it immediately. In practice judgement may be applied at any of the following stages:

● Judgement as to whether an information area is relevant to the matter under consideration. This precedes the development of any ideas.

● Judgement as to the validity of an idea in one's own internal thinking process. Dismissing such an idea instead of exploring it.

● Judgement as to its correctness before offering an idea to others.

● Judgement of an idea offered by someone else – either in refusing to accept it or in actual condemnation of it.

In this regard judgement, evaluation and criticism are regarded as similar processes. Suspension of judgement does not imply suspension of condemnation – it implies suspension of judgement whether the outcome is favourable or otherwise.

The suspension of judgement can have the following effects:

● An idea will survive longer and will breed further ideas.

● Other people will offer ideas which their own judgement would have rejected. Such ideas may be extremely useful to those receiving them.

● The ideas of others can be accepted for their stimulating effect instead of being rejected.

● Ideas which are judged to be wrong within the current frame of reference may survive long enough to show that the frame of reference needs altering.

In the diagram below A is the starting point of a problem. In tackling the problem one moves towards K but this idea is unsound and so it is rejected. Instead one moves towards C. But from C one can go nowhere. Had one moved towards K then one could have proceeded from there to G and from G to B which is the solution. Once one had reached B then one would have been able to see the correct path from A through P.

Practical application

The principle of suspended judgement has been discussed. The practical application of this principle needs outlining for it is not much use accepting the principle but never applying it. In practice the principle leads to the following behaviour:

● One does not rush to judge or evaluate an idea. One does not regard judgement or evaluation as the most important thing that can be done to an idea. One prefers exploration.

● Some ideas are obviously wrong even when no attempt at judgement is made. In such cases one shifts attention from why it is wrong to how it can be useful.

● Even if one knows that an idea must eventually be thrown out one delays that moment in order to extract as much usefulness from the idea as possible.

● Instead of forcing an idea in the direction which judgement indicates, one follows along behind it.

A bucket with holes cannot carry much water. One could reject it out of hand. Or one could see how far it could carry how much water. In spite of the holes it may be very useful for bringing about a certain effect.

In so far as it is not just a matter of copying, design requires a good deal of innovation. Design is a convenient format for practising the lateral thinking principles that have been discussed up to this point. The design process itself is discussed at length in a later section; in this section design is used as practice for lateral thinking.

Practice

The designs are to be visual and in black and white or colour. Verbal descriptions can be added to the pictures to explain certain features or to explain how they work. The advantages of a visual format are many.

1. There has to be a definite commitment to a way of doing something rather than a vague generalized description.

2. The design is expressed in a manner that is visible to everyone.

3. Visual expression of a complicated structure is much easier than verbal expression. It would be a pity to limit design by the ability to describe it.

The designs could be worked out as a classroom exercise or they could be done as homework. It is easier if the students all work on the same design rather than on individual choices for then any comments apply to them all, there is more comparison and they are all more involved in the analysis.

It is convenient if all the designs are executed on standard-sized sheets of paper. Once the design task has been set no additional information is given. No attempt is made to make the design project more specific. 'Do whatever you think is best' is the answer to any question.

● Comment on results

Unless the group is small enough to actually cluster around the drawings these would have to be copied and shown on an overhead projector or epidiascope. Or they could just be pinned up. Adequate discussion could be carried out without showing the drawings at all but just redrawing the important features on the blackboard. In commenting on the results the teacher would want to bear the following points in mind:

1. Resist the temptation to judge. Resist the temptation to say, 'this would not work because . . .'

2. Resist the temptation to choose one way of doing things as being much better than any other for fear of polarizing design in one direction.

3. Emphasize the variety of the different ways of carrying out a particular function. List the different suggestions and add others of one's own.

4. Try and look at the function underlying a particular design. Try to separate the intention of the designer from the actual way this was carried out.

5. Note the features that have been put there for a functional purpose and the ones that are there as ornaments to complete the picture.

6. Question certain points – not in order to destroy them but in order to find out if there was any special reason behind them which may not be manifest.

7. Note the borrowing of complete designs from what might have been seen on television, in the cinema or in comics.

● Suggestions

Design projects can either ask for improvements on existing things or for the actual invention of something to carry out a task. It is easiest if the designs do involve something physical since this is easier to draw. They do not have to be mechanical in the strictest sense of the word; for instance the design of a new classroom or a new type of shoe would be very suitable. It is enough that they are concrete projects. In addition one can try organizational designs. Organizational designs would ask for ways of doing things such as building a house very quickly.

Design:
An apple picking machine.
A potato peeling machine.
A cart to go over rough ground.
A cup that cannot spill.
A machine to dig tunnels.
A device to help cars to park.

Redesign:
The human body.
A new milk bottle.
A chair.
A school.
A new type of clothes.
A better umbrella.

Organizational:
How to build a house very quickly.
How to arrange the checkout counters in a supermarket.
How to organize garbage collection.
How to organize shopping to take up the least time.
How to put a drain across a busy road.

● Variety

The purpose of the design session is to show that there can be different ways of doing something. It is not the individual designs that matter so much as the comparison between designs. In order to show this variety one could compare the complete designs but it is more effective to pick out some particular function and show how this was handled by the different designers. For instance in the design of an apple picking machine one could choose the function of 'reaching the apples'. To reach the apples some students will have used extendable arms, others will have raised the whole vehicle on jacks, others will have tried to bring the apples to the ground, others might have planted the trees in trenches anyway. For each function the teacher lists the different methods used and asks for further suggestions. He can also add suggestions of his own or ones derived from previous experience with the design project.

Particular functions with the apple picking machine could include the following:
Reaching the apples.
Finding the apples.
Picking the apples.
Transporting the apples to the ground.
Sorting out the apples.
Putting the apples in containers.
Moving on to the next tree.

It is not suggested that in carrying out the design the student will have tried to cover all these functions. Most of them would be covered quite unconsciously. Nevertheless one can consciously analyse what has been done and show the different ways of doing it. In many cases no provision will have been made for carrying out a certain function (e.g. transporting the apples to the ground). In such cases one does not criticize the designs that do not show the function but commends those that do show it.

● Evaluation

One could criticize designs for omissions, for errors of mechanics, for errors of efficiency, for errors of magnitude and for all sorts of other errors. It is difficult to resist the temptation to do this – but the temptation must be resisted.

If some designs have left things out then one shows this up by commenting on those designs which have put it in.

If some design shows an arrangement that is mechanically unsound then one comments on the function intended rather than on the particular way of carrying it out.

If some designs show a very roundabout way of doing something one describes the design without criticism and then describes more efficient designs.

One of the most common faults with designs by students in the 10–13 age group is the tendency to lose sight of the design project and to go into great detail drawing some vehicle that is derived directly from another source such as television or space comics. Thus an apple picking machine will be shown bristling with guns, rockets, radar and jets. Details will be given about number of crew, speed, range, power, how much it would cost to build, how long it would take to build, how many nuts and bolts, the materials used in construction and so on. There is no point in criticizing the superfluity of all this. Instead one emphasizes the functional economy and effectiveness of other designs.

It is important not to criticize actual mechanics. One designer of an apple picking machine suggested putting bits of metal in each of the apples and then using powerful magnets buried in the ground under each tree to pull the apples down. It would be easy to criticize this as follows:

1. Just as much trouble to put bits of metal in each apple as to pick each one directly.

2. The magnet would have to be very powerful indeed to pull the apples down from such a distance.

3. The apples would be badly damaged on hitting the ground.

4. Buried magnets would only be able to collect apples from one tree.

These are all valid comments and one could make many more. But rather than criticizing in this manner one could say: 'Here is someone who instead of going up to pick the apples like everybody else wants to attract the apples to the ground. Instead of having to find the apples and then to pick them one by one he can get them all together and all at once.' Both these are very valid points. The actual method for carrying out the function is obviously inefficient but it is better to let that be than to appear to criticize the concept of function by criticizing the way it is carried out. When that particular designer learns more about magnets he will find that they would not be much good. At the moment however they represent the only method he knows for carrying out 'attraction from a distance'.

In another design for a cart that would go over rough ground the designer suggested some sort of 'smooth stuff' that was sucked

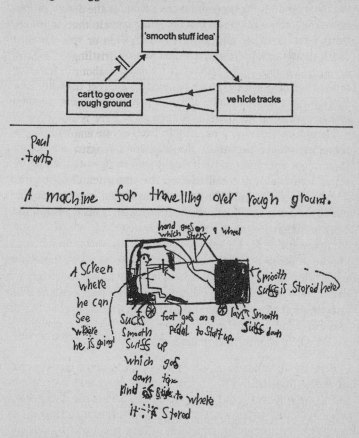

up by the cart from behind itself and then spread down in front of it. Thus the cart was always travelling over smooth stuff. There was even a reservoir for evening out the supply of the smooth stuff. It would be easy to criticize the idea as follows:

1. What sort of 'smooth stuff' would fill in big hollows? One would need far too much.

2. One could never suck back all that had been laid down and so the supply would run out after a few feet.

3. The cart would have to move very slowly indeed.

Such criticisms are easy but instead one would appreciate that the designer had got away from the usual approach of providing special wheels or other devices for going over rough ground and instead was trying to alter the *ground itself*. From such a concept could come the notion of a tracked vehicle which does actually lay down smooth stuff and pick it up again. There are also those military vehicles which have a roll of steel mesh or glass fibre matting on their backs and this is laid down ahead of the vehicle to make a road on which the vehicle then runs.

Though an idea may seem silly in itself it can still lead to something useful. As shown in the diagram the smooth stuff idea though not a solution in itself might lead straight to the idea of a tracked vehicle. If one had rejected the smooth stuff idea then it might have been harder to get to the same point. The attitude is not, 'This won't work, let's throw it out' but, 'This is not going to work but what does it lead us to?'

No one is silly for the sake of being silly no matter how it might appear to other people. There must be a reason why something made sense to the person who drew it at the moment when it was drawn. What it appears to other people is not so important if one is trying to encourage lateral thinking. In any case whatever the reason behind a design and however silly it may be it can still be a most useful stimulus to further ideas.

● Assumptions

In the design process there is a tendency to use 'complete units'. This means that when one borrows a unit from somewhere else in order to carry out some special function that unit is used 'complete'. Thus a mechanical arm to pick apples will have five fingers because the human arm has that number. In an attempt to break up such complete units and isolate what is really required one can question the assumption behind them: 'Why does a hand need five fingers to pick apples?'

One may also question assumptions that seem to be basic to the design itself.

Why do we have to *pick* the apples off the trees?

Why do trees have to be that shape?

Why does the arm have to go up and down with every apple it picks?

Some of the points challenged could easily have been taken for granted. By challenging them one can open up new ideas. For instance one could shake apples from trees instead of picking them. In California, they are experimenting with growing trees in a special way which would make it possible to pick the fruit more easily. The arm does not need to go up and down with each apple; the apples could be dropped into a chute or container.

The 'why' technique can be applied to any part of the design project. To begin with the teacher would apply it after discussing the designs. The students could also apply it to their own designs or those of others. As usual the purpose of the 'why' technique is not to try and justify something but to see what happens when one challenges the uniqueness of a particular way of doing things.

Summary

The design process is a convenient format for developing the idea of lateral thinking. The emphasis is on the *different* ways of doing things, the *different* ways of looking at things and the escape from cliché concepts, the challenging of assumptions. Critical evaluation is temporarily suspended in order to develop a generative frame of mind in which flexibility and variety can be used with confidence. For the design session to work it is essential that the person running it understands the purpose of the session. It is not practice in design but practice in lateral thinking.

There is nothing vague about a geometrical shape. As a situation it is very definite – one knows what one is looking at. Most situations however are much more vague than this. Most of the time one has a vague awareness of the situation and nothing more. With a definite geometrical shape it is easy to think of alternative ways of dividing it up and alternative ways of putting the pieces together again. It is much more difficult to do this if there is only a vague awareness of the situation.

Everyone is confident that they know what they are talking about, reading about or writing about but if you ask them to pick out the dominant idea there is difficulty in doing so. It is difficult to convert a vague awareness into a definite statement. The statement is either too long and complicated or else it leaves out too much. Sometimes the different aspects of the subject do not hang together to give a single theme.

Unless one can convert a vague awareness to a definite pattern it is extremely difficult to generate alternative patterns, alternative ways of looking at the situation. In a defining situation one picks out the dominant idea not in order to be frozen by that idea but in order to be able to generate alternative ideas.

Unless one can pick out the dominant idea one is going to be dominated by it. Whatever way one tries to look at the situation is likely to be dominated by the ever present but undefined dominant idea. One of the main purposes of picking out the dominant idea is to be able to escape from it. One can more easily escape from something definite than from something vague. Liberation from rigid patterns and the generation of alternative patterns are the aims of lateral thinking. Both processes are made much easier if one can pick out the dominant idea.

If one cannot pick out the dominant idea then any alternatives one generates are likely to be imprisoned within that vague general idea. The diagram below shows how one may feel that one is generating an alternative point of view and yet this is still within the same framework of the dominant idea as the original point of view. It is only when one becomes aware of the framework that one can generate an alternative point of view outside of it.

The dominant idea resides not in the situation itself but in the way it is looked at. Some people seem much better at picking out the dominant idea. Some people seem much better at crystallizing the situation in a single sentence. This may be because they can separate the main idea from the detail or it may be because they tend to have a simpler view of things. In order to be able to pick out the dominant idea one must make a conscious effort to do so and one needs practice.

Different dominant ideas

If students are asked to pick out the dominant idea from a newspaper article there are usually several different versions of what the dominant idea is. From an article on parks the following may be chosen as the dominant idea:

The beauty of parkland.

The value of parkland as a contrast to the city surroundings.

The need to develop more parks.

The difficulty of developing or preserving parks.

Parkland as a relaxation or pleasure.

The author is exercising the function of protest and parkland happens to be a suitable theme.

The danger of the demands of urban growth.

These are all different but related ideas. It is easy to say that some of the ideas are more truly dominant than others and yet to the person picking out the idea this idea has a valid dominance. It is not a matter of finding *the* dominant idea but of getting into the habit of trying to pick out the dominant idea. It is not a matter of analysing the situation but of seeing it clearly enough to be able to generate different points of view. It is not a matter of making use of the dominant idea but of identifying it in order to avoid it.

In the design situation discussed in the preceding section the organizing effect of the dominant idea is quite obvious. The dominant idea is never actually stated but for different groups the idea is different. When children try to design a machine for picking apples the dominant idea is 'reaching the apples'. The children think in personal terms which involve wanting one apple at a time and also the difficulty (for a small child) of actually reaching the apples. When the same design problem is given to an industrial engineering group the dominant idea is 'effectiveness in commercial terms'. This is a wide concept which includes speed and cheapness of operation without any damage to the apples. From this point of view reaching the apples is not so much a problem as finding them, picking many at a time, bringing them to the ground without damage, and all this with a cheap machine that can easily be moved from tree to tree. In short the dominant problem for the engineers is 'advantage over manual labour' whereas for the children it is 'getting the apples'.

Hierarchy of dominant ideas

As soon as one starts picking out dominant ideas one becomes aware that there are different degrees of comprehensiveness of dominant ideas. The dominant idea may include the whole subject or only one aspect of it. Thus from an article on crime one might pick out the following dominant ideas:
Crime.
Behaviour of people.
Violence.
Social structures and crime.
The trend of crime.
What can be done.

Clearly 'crime' and 'the behaviour of people' are much wider ideas than 'violence' or 'what can be done' but all of them are valid dominant ideas. There is a hierarchy which extends upwards from the more specific ideas to the more general. In picking out the dominant idea it is not a matter of searching for the most general and most comprehensive idea for this may be so very wide that it is impossible to move outside it at all. In picking out a dominant idea it is not a matter of having to justify to someone else that the idea is *the dominant idea* which covers the whole situation and which cannot therefore be challenged. It is a matter of picking out an idea which seems (to oneself) to dominate the issue. For instance in the article on crime the dominant idea might have seemed to be 'the uncertainty about the value of punishment' or 'the protection of the rights of a citizen even if he was a criminal'.

Crucial factor

A dominant idea is the organizing theme in a way of looking at a situation. It is often present but undefined and one tries to define it in order to escape from it. A crucial factor is some element of the situation which must always be included no matter how one looks at the situation. The crucial factor is a tethering point. Like a dominant idea a crucial factor can immobilize a situation and make it impossible to shift a point of view. Like a dominant idea a crucial factor may exert a powerful influence without ever being consciously recognized.

The difference between a dominant idea and a crucial factor is shown diagrammatically below. The dominant idea organizes the situation. The crucial factor tethers it and though some mobility is allowed this is restricted.

dominant idea

crucial factor

The purpose of isolating crucial factors is to examine them. Very often a crucial factor is an assumption – at least the 'crucial' nature of that factor is an assumption. Once the factor is isolated one challenges the necessity for it. If the factor is found not to be crucial then the tethering effect of that factor disappears and there is more freedom in structuring the situation in a different way. In the design of a machine for picking apples a crucial factor may have been 'that the apples must not be damaged' or 'that only ripe apples were to be picked'. The necessity to include such crucial factors would restrict the way the problem could be looked at. For instance shaking the tree would not be a good idea.

There may be one crucial factor, several crucial factors or none at all. Different people may choose different crucial factors. As with finding the dominant idea what matters is that one identifies what seems to be a crucial factor in one's own view of the problem. Whether it really is crucial or whether other people would think so does not matter for one picks it out only to challenge its necessity.

In looking for the dominant idea one wants to know, 'why are we always looking at this thing in the same way?' In looking for the crucial factor one wants to know, 'what is holding us up, what is keeping us to this old approach?'

In itself the search for dominant ideas or crucial factors is not a lateral thinking process at all. It is a necessary step which allows one to use lateral thinking more effectively. It is difficult to restructure a pattern unless one can see the pattern. It is difficult to loosen up a pattern unless one can identify the rigid points.

Practice

1. A newspaper article is read out to the students who then have to note down:
   (1). The dominant idea (or ideas).
   (2). The crucial factors.

When the results have been collected the teacher goes through them and lists the different choices. A person making a particular choice may be asked to explain why he made that choice. This is not in order that the choice be justified or in order to show that it was not as good as other choices but in order to elaborate a particular point of view. There is no attempt to disqualify any of the choices or to rank them in order of excellence.

If it is clear that some of the students have not grasped the point about dominant ideas and crucial factors then one concentrates on those answers which make the point most clearly. If none of them do then the teacher has to supply his own choice of dominant idea and crucial factor for the passage used.

It is not a good idea to ask for choices of dominant ideas and then to list them on the blackboard as was suggested in previous sections. This is because a choice which seems to be very good will inhibit any further suggestions. It is far better to let people work out what seems dominant or crucial to them and then to show the variety of answers.

2. Radio or tape recorder

Instead of the teacher reading the passage out it could be a feature programme on the radio or something taped off the radio. The advantage of a tape recording is its repeatability.

3. Instead of listening to a passage being read out the students can be given passages to study for themselves. This is rather different since there is more time to go over the piece, the interpretation is not so determined by the way it has been read out and one can go back and reexamine what has been written to see if it supports a particular point of view.

4. Discussion

Two students are asked to debate a subject in front of the class. One can either choose students who declare they have opposite views on a particular subject or else ask the students to debate from opposite points of view whether or not they hold those views. The rest of the class listens to the debate and notes down the dominant idea and crucial factors in the discussion. In order to try and check the validity of these the other students can ask the debaters questions.

5. Design project

Either in the course of a design project or in discussing the results of a design project undertaken by others the students can try and pick out the dominant ideas and crucial factors. In this case they can examine the crucial factors to see whether they really are crucial and to see what would happen if one did not include them in the design. The same thing could be done with dominant ideas: the students first picking out the ideas and then seeing how they could escape them.

Although it would be easy to combine this sort of practice session with the lateral thinking processes described before (and those to be described later) it is probably better not to do so. If one were to combine the process of generating alternatives with the process of picking out the dominant idea then there is a tendency to pick out a dominant idea which fits nicely in with the alternative one can think of. The choice of dominant ideas and crucial factors soon becomes tailored to show how clever one is at avoiding them. For the moment it is enough to become skilled at finding dominant ideas and crucial factors.

The aim of lateral thinking is to look at things in different ways, to restructure patterns, to generate alternatives. The mere intention of generating alternatives is sometimes sufficient. Such an intention can make one pause and look around before proceeding too far with the obvious way of looking at the situation. As one looks around one may find that there are other alternatives waiting to be considered. At other times the mere intention of generating alternatives is not sufficient. Goodwill cannot by itself generate alternatives. One has to use some more practical method. For the same reason exhorting people to look for alternatives does have a certain usefulness (especially in tempering the arrogance of a unique point of view) but one also needs to develop ways of generating alternatives.

In the self-maximizing memory system of mind there is a tendency for established patterns to grow larger and larger. The patterns may grow by extension or else two separate patterns may join up to form a large single one. This tendency of patterns to grow larger is seen clearly with language. Words describing individual features are put together to describe a new situation which soon acquires its own language label. Once this has happened a new standard pattern has been formed. This new pattern is used in its own right without constant reference to the original features which made up the pattern.

The more unified a pattern the more difficult it is to restructure it. Thus when a single standard pattern takes over from a collection of smaller patterns the situation becomes much more difficult to look at in a new way. In order to make such restructuring easier one tries to return to the collection of smaller patterns. If a child is given a complete doll's house he has little choice but to use and admire it as it is. If however he is given a box of building blocks then he can assemble them in different ways to give a variety of houses.

Above is shown a geometrical shape which could be described as an 'L shape'. The problem is to divide this shape into four pieces which are exactly similar in size, shape and area. Initial attempts to do this usually take the form of the divisions shown on the left.

These are obviously inadequate since the pieces are not the same in size even though they may be the same in shape.

A correct solution is shown on p. 117 on the right and it is seen to consist of four small L-shaped pieces. An easy way to reach this answer is to divide the original shape into three squares and then to divide each of these into four pieces which gives a total of twelve pieces. These twelve pieces must then be assembled in four groups of three and when this has been accomplished as shown, the original is divided into the required four pieces.

One of the problems set in a previous chapter asked for a square to be divided into four pieces which were the same in size, shape and area. Some people went further than the usual obvious divisions by dividing the square into sixteen small squares and then reassembling them in different ways to give a variety of new ways of dividing the square into four.

In a sense the whole point of language is to give separate units that can be moved around and put together in different ways. The danger is that these different ways soon become established as fixed units themselves and not as temporary arrangements of other units.

If one takes any situation and breaks it down into fractions one can then restructure the situation by putting the fractions together in a new way.

True and false divisions

It might seem that what is being recommended is the analysis of a situation into its component parts. This is not so. One is not trying to *find* the true component parts of a situation, one is trying to *create* parts. The natural or true lines of division are usually not much good as the parts tend to reassemble to give the original pattern since this is how the pattern came about in the first place. With artificial divisions however there is more opportunity to put units together in novel ways. As is so often the case with lateral thinking one is looking for a provocative arrangement of information that can lead to a new way of looking at things. One is not trying to discover the *correct* way. What one needs is something to be going on with and for this purpose any sort of fractionation will do.

In the design of an apple picking machine the problem could have been fractionated into the following parts:
reaching
finding
picking
transport to the ground
undamaged apples.

In reassembling these fractions one might have put reaching-finding-picking together and then substituted shaking the tree for all these functions. One would then be left with transport to the ground in such a way that the apples were not damaged. On the other hand one might have put reaching-undamaged apples-transport to the ground together and come up with some elevated canvas platform which would be raised towards the apples.

Someone else might have fractionated the problem in a different way:
contribution of tree to apple picking
contribution of apples
contribution of machine

This particular type of fractionation might have led on to the idea of growing the trees in a special way that would make it easier to pick the apples.

Complete division and overlap

Since the purpose of fractionation is to break up the solid unity of a fixed pattern rather than to provide a descriptive analysis it does not matter if the fractions do not cover the whole situation. It is enough that one has something to work with. It is enough that one has a new arrangement of information to provoke restructuring of the original pattern.

For the same reason it does not matter if some of the fractions overlap. It is much better to produce some sort of fractionation no matter how impure than to sit wondering how a pure fractionation can be made.

If the problem being considered was 'transport by bus' the following fractionation might be made:

Choice of route.

Frequency.

Convenience.

Number of people using the service.

Number of people using the service at different times.

Size of bus.

Economics of use and cost.

Alternative transport.

Number of people who would have to use the bus and number who would like to use it if it were running.

Clearly these fractions are not all separate but overlap to a considerable extent, for instance convenience is a matter of route, frequency and perhaps size of the bus. Economics of use and cost include the number of people using the service, size of bus and several other of the fractions.

Two unit division

Whenever there is difficulty in dividing something into fractions it can be useful to adopt the *artificial* technique of division into two units or fractions. The two fractions so produced are them-

selves further divided into two more fractions and so on until one has a satisfactory number of fractions.

This technique is highly artificial and it can mean that several important features are quite overlooked. The advantage is that it is much easier to find two fractions than to find several. It is not a question of dividing something into two equal fractions for any two fractions will do no matter how unequal. Nor do the lines of division have to reveal natural fractions. The fractions may be very artificial and yet be useful.

Applied to the apple picking problem the two unit division might go as follows:

apple picking problem	apple	delicate	damaging
			damaged
			finding
		separate	density
			hold
	picking	remove	jerk
			to ground
		transport	container

The technique of two unit division is not so much a technique but a method for encouraging the fractionation of a situation.

Practice

1. Fractionation
The students are given a subject and asked to fractionate it. The subject may be a design project, a problem or any specific theme. Suggestions for subjects might include:
Unloading ships in habour.
Restaurant meals.
Catching and marketing of fish.
Organization of a football league.
Building a bridge.
Newspapers.

The separate fractionation lists are collected from the students. If there is time the results are analysed in terms of the most popular fractions. If there is not time then individual lists are read out and particularly ingenious fractionations are commented upon. The main purpose is to show the variety or the uniformity of the approach.

2. Reassembly

From the fractionation lists obtained above (or from a special session) are extracted small groups of two or three fractions. These are then given to the students who are asked to put them together again in an attempt to generate a new way of looking at the situation.

3. Picking out fractions

Here the subject is presented to the students as a group. They are asked to pick out fractions one after the other. One student volunteers one fraction and then another student follows with a further fraction. This continues as long as suggestions are still coming in. It does not matter if there is a considerable degree of overlap between the suggested fractions. If there seems to be a direct duplication this is pointed out to the person making the suggestion and he is asked to say why he thinks there is a difference. It does not matter whether the difference is a very valid one or not so long as he himself seems to think there is a difference.

4. Working backwards.

This is as much a game as anything else. A list of fractions is taken from a previous session with another group and the students are asked to try and guess what the subject was. Obvious references to the subject are deleted and substituted by the word 'blank'.

Another way in which this can be done is to give the students a list of five subjects only one of which is to be fractionated by each student. At the end some of the fraction lists are read out and the students have to decide which of the five original subjects a list refers to.

5. Two unit division

Here a subject is given to the students who are asked to carry out a two unit division on it. The end results are then compared. A quick comparison can be made between the first two units chosen by the different students. This can serve to show the variety of approaches used by the different students.

6. Sequential two unit division

A subject is given and then one student is asked to divide it

into two units. Then another student is required to divide one of
the units into two further units and so on. Unlike other practice
sessions this one is not a matter of volunteering a solution but of
being asked to provide one. The intention is to show that it is
always possible to divide something into two units by picking
out one unit and having the remainder as the other unit.

Summary

Fractionation may seem to be no more than straightforward
analysis. The emphasis is however quite different. The aim is not
to provide a complete or true breakdown of the situation into its
component parts (as in analysis) but to provide material which
can be used to stimulate restructuring of the original situation.
The aim is restructuring not explanation. The fractions do not
have to be complete or natural for the emphasis is not on whether
they are valid but on what they can bring about. The purpose of
fractionation is to escape from the inhibiting unity of a fixed
pattern to the more generative situation of several fractions.

Fractionation is a useful method for generating alternative ways of looking at a situation. But it has certain limitations. The fractions chosen are themselves fixed patterns and usually standard patterns. The choice of fractions is usually a vertical choice which follows the most natural lines of division. The result is that the fractions come together again to give a standard view of the situation. Although fractionation makes it easier to look at a situation in a different way the actual choice of fractions limits the variety of alternatives that can be generated. A simple square shape is shown opposite. If one had to break this down into fractions one might choose the fractions shown in any of the other figures. Yet the choice of fraction will determine the shape that can be made by reassembling the fractions differently.

The reversal method is more lateral in nature than the fractionation one. It tends to produce more unusual restructuring.

If you give someone an open-ended creative problem there is great difficulty in getting started. There is difficulty in moving at all. The person presented with the problem seems to say, 'Where do I go, what do I do?' This was very obvious when I asked a group of people to redesign some feature of the human body. One obvious approach was to take some actual feature as a starting point and then to modify it in some simple way. Thus there were suggestions to increase the number of arms or to lengthen the arms or to make them more flexible.

Unless one is going to sit around waiting for inspiration the most practical way to get moving is to work on what one has. In a swimming race when the swimmers come to turn at the end of the pool they kick hard against the end to increase their speed. In the reversal method one kicks hard against what is there and fixed in order to move away in the opposite direction.

Wherever a direction is indicated then the opposite direction is equally well defined. If you go towards New York you are going away from London (or whatever other place you started from). Whenever there is action then the opposite action is indicated. If you are filling a bath full of water then the opposite action is to empty the bath. If something is happening over time then one merely runs the time scale backwards in order to find the reverse process. This is rather like running a ciné film backwards. Whenever there is a one way relationship between two parties the situation can be reversed by changing the direction of this relationship. If a person is supposed to obey the government then the reversal would imply that the government ought to obey a person (or people).

In the reversal method one takes things as they are and then turns them round, inside out, upside down, back to front. Then one sees what happens. It is a provocative rearrangement of information. You make water run uphill instead of downhill. Instead of driving a car the car leads you.

Different types of reversal

There are usually several different ways in which one can 'reverse' a given situation. There is no one correct way. Nor should there be any search for some true reversal. Any sort of reversal will do.

For instance if the situation is, 'a policeman organizing traffic', then the following reversals might be made:
The traffic organizes (controls) the policeman.
The policeman disorganizes the traffic.

Which of these reversals is the better one? Either will do. It is impossible to say which arrangement will be the more useful until it has proved so. It is not a matter of choosing the more reasonable reversal or the more unreasonable one. One is searching for alternatives, for change, for provocative arrangements of information.

In lateral thinking one is not looking for the right answer but for a different arrangement of information which will provoke a different way of looking at the situation.

The purpose of the reversal procedure

Very often the reversal procedure leads to a way of looking at the situation that is obviously wrong or ridiculous. What then is the point of doing it?
● One uses the reversal procedure in order to escape from the absolute necessity to look at the situation in the standard way. It does not matter whether the new way makes sense or not for once one escapes then it becomes easier to move in other directions as well.

● By disrupting the original way of looking at the situation one frees information that can come together in a new way.

● To overcome the terror of being wrong, of taking a step that is not fully justified.

● The main purpose is provocative. By making the reversal one moves to a new position. Then one sees what happens.

● Occasionally the reversed approach is useful in itself.

With the policeman situation the first reversal supposed that the traffic was controlling the policeman. This would lead to consideration of the demand for more policemen as traffic became more complex, the need for redistribution of policemen according to traffic conditions. It would make one realize that in fact the traffic does actually control the policeman since his behaviour depends on the traffic build up in different roads. How quickly does he react to this? How sensitive is he to this? How well informed can he be of this? Since the traffic is controlling the policeman who is controlling the traffic why not organize things so that the traffic controlled itself?

The second reversal in the policeman situation supposed that the policeman was disorganizing the traffic. This would lead to a consideration of whether natural flow, traffic lights or a policeman was most efficient. If a policeman was more efficient than the lights, what was the added factor – could this be built into the lights? Was it perhaps easier for the traffic to adjust to fixed patterns of direction rather than to the unpredictable reactions of the policeman?

A flock of sheep was moving slowly down a country lane which was bounded by high banks. A motorist in a hurry came up behind the flock and urged the shepherd to move his sheep to the side so that the car could drive through. The shepherd refused since he could not be sure of keeping all the sheep out of the way of the car in such a narrow lane. Instead he reversed the situation. He told the car to stop and then he quietly turned the flock round and drove it back past the stationary car.

In Aesop's fable the water in the jug was at too low a level for the bird to drink. The bird was thinking of taking water out of the jug but instead he thought of putting something in. So he dropped pebbles into the jug until the level of water rose high enough for him to drink.

The duchess was much overweight. Physician after physician tried to reduce her weight by putting her on a near starvation diet and each physician was in turn dismissed on account of the unpleasantness of the diet. At last there came a physician who fussed over the good lady. Unlike the others he told her that she was not eating enough to sustain her huge body. He recommended that she drink a glass of sweetened milk half-an-hour before all meals (which of course reduced her appetite very much).

The rich man wanted his daughter to marry the richest of her suitors. But the daughter was in love with a poor student. So she went to her father and said that she wanted to marry the richest of her suitors but how could they tell which was the richest. It would be no use asking them to show their wealth by giving a present since it would be easy to borrow money for this purpose if the daughter was to be the prize. Instead she suggested that her father should give a present of money to each of the suitors. Then one would be able to tell how rich each was by the difference that the present of money made to their usual way of life. The father praised her for her wisdom and gave a present to each suitor. Whereupon the daughter eloped with her now enriched true love.

In each of these examples a simple reversal proved useful in itself. More often reversals are not especially useful in themselves but only in what they lead to. One ought to get into the habit of reversing situations and then seeing what happens. If nothing happens then there is no loss and there must be some gain in the challenge to the established way of looking at things.

Practice

1. Reversal and different types of reversal

A number of situations are presented to the students each of whom has to try reversing each situation in as many ways as possible. The results are collected and then the different types of reversal are listed. Comments are made on the more obvious types and also on the more ingenious types.

The same thing can also be done by giving out a subject and then asking for volunteer reversals of it, listing these down on a blackboard as they come in (and supplementing them with one's own suggestions).

Possible subjects might be:
Teacher instructing students.
Street cleaner.
Milkman delivering milk.
Going on holiday.
Workers striking.
Shop assistants helping customers.

Comment

In some cases the reversal may seem utterly ridiculous. This does not matter. It is just as useful to practise being ridiculous as to practise reversal. In the above examples (and the teacher can generate different ones) it is not just a matter of reversing the given statement but of reversing some aspect of the subject itself. For instance 'going on holiday' can be reversed as 'holiday coming to one'. On the other hand one might consider a holiday as 'a change of scenery' and reverse this to a holiday as 'complete uniformity of surroundings'.

2. What reversal leads to

Here one takes the situation and its reversal and sees what the reversal leads to. This is best done in a general classroom situation. The situation and its reversal are offered to the class and volunteer suggestions are invited as to lines of thought that the reversal might open up. For instance the idea that 'holidays might involve complete uniformity of surroundings' might lead to the idea of freedom from decision, from stress, from having to adapt.

To begin with it is not always easy to develop further ideas from the reversed situation. That is why it is better to do it in an open class situation rather than require each student to work out something for himself. Once the idea is grasped and everyone seems eager to offer suggestions then each individual student can be asked to reverse a situation and develop lines of thought that arise from that reversal. In considering and commenting on these at the end it is necessary to be able to trace the line of development of an idea rather than just have the end product. For that reason the students ought to be encouraged to put down their train of thought.

What has been discussed so far includes the general principles of lateral thinking and special techniques for practising these principles and applying them. Brainstorming is a formal *setting* for the use of lateral thinking. In itself it is not a special technique but a special setting which encourages the application of the principles and techniques of lateral thinking while providing a holiday from the rigidity of vertical thinking.

The previous sections have described techniques that could be used on one's own. The practice sessions have involved a teacher-student interaction. Brainstorming is a group activity. Nor does it require any teacher intervention.

The main features of a brainstorming session are:

● Cross stimulation.

● Suspended judgement.

● The formality of the setting.

Cross stimulation

The fractionation technique and the reversal technique are methods for getting ideas moving. One needs to move to a new arrangement of information and then one can carry on from there. The new arrangement of information is a provocation which produces some effect. In a brainstorming session the provocation is supplied by the ideas of others. Since such ideas come from outside one's own mind they can serve to stimulate one's own ideas. Even if one misunderstands the idea it can still be a useful stimulus. It often happens that an idea may seem very obvious and trivial to one person and yet it can combine with other ideas in someone else's mind to produce something very original. In a brainstorming session one gives out stimulation to others and one receives it from others. Because the different people taking part each tend to follow their own lines of thought there is less danger of getting stuck with a particular way of looking at the situation.

During the brainstorming session the ideas are recorded by a notetaker and perhaps by a tape recorder as well. These ideas can then be played back at a later date in order to provide fresh stimulation. Although the ideas themselves are not new the context has changed so the old ideas can have a new stimulating effect.

Although the ideas in a brainstorming session are related to the problem under discussion they can still act as random stimuli for they can be far removed from the idea pattern of the person listening to them. The value of random stimulation is discussed in a later section.

Suspended judgement

The value of suspended judgement has been discussed in a previous section. The brainstorming session provides a formal opportunity for people to make suggestions that they would not otherwise dare make for fear of being laughed at. In a brainstorming session anything goes. No idea is too ridiculous to be put forward. It is important that no attempt at evaluation of ideas is made during the brainstorming session.

Attempts at evaluation might include such remarks as:
'That would never work because . . .'
'But what would you do about . . .'
'It is well-known that . . .'
'That has already been tried and found to be no good.'
'How would you get that to . . .'

'You are leaving a vital point out of consideration.'
'That is a silly, impractical idea.'
'That would be much too expensive.'
'No one would accept that.'

These are very natural remarks but if they are allowed then the brainstorming session is useless. Not only is one forbidden to evaluate the ideas of others but also one's own ideas. It is the job of the chairman of the session to stop any attempts at evaluation. He must make this quite clear at the start of the session.

Thereafter he need only say : 'That is evaluation,' in order to put a stop to it.

The other type of evaluation which must be guarded against is the evaluation of the novelty of an idea. The object of a brainstorming session is to produce *effective* ideas. Usually this means new ideas. otherwise one would not be holding the session. But the purpose of the session is not actually to find *new ideas*. During the session a long forgotten idea may be resurrected and found to be very effective.

The evaluation of novelty might include such remarks as :
'That is not new.'
'I remember reading about that some time ago.'
'That has already been tried in America.'
'That was the way it was done years ago.'
'I thought of that myself but threw it out.'
'What is so original about that idea?'

To counter such tendencies the chairman has to say, 'Never mind how new it is, let's have the idea and worry about its novelty later.'

Formality of the setting

Lateral thinking is an attitude of mind, a type of thinking. It is not a special technique, much less a formal setting. Yet the value of a brainstorming session lies in the formality of the setting. The more formal the setting the better. The more formal the setting the more chance there is of informality in ideas within it. Most people are so steeped in vertical thinking habits that they feel very inhibited about lateral thinking. They do not like being wrong or ridiculous even though they might accept the generative value of this. The more *special* the brainstorming session is the more chance there is of the participants leaving their inhibitions outside. It is much easier to accept that 'anything goes' as a way of thinking in a brainstorming session than as a way of thinking in general.

Within this formal setting one can use all the other techniques that have been described so far for restructuring patterns and also those techniques which are yet to be described. One can try dividing things up into fractions and putting these together in new ways. One can try reversal. One does not have to apologize for it or even explain it to the others. The formality of the session gives one the licence to do what one likes with one's own thoughts without reference to the criticism of others.

Format for brainstorming session

● Size

There is no ideal size. Twelve people is a convenient number but a brainstorming session can work very well with as many as fifteen or as few as six. Less than six usually becomes an argument and with more than fifteen each person does not get enough opportunity to contribute. If there is a larger group then it can be broken down into smaller groups and notes can be compared at the end.

● Chairman

It is the chairman's job to guide the session without in any way controlling or directing it. He has the following duties:

1. The chairman stops people trying to evaluate or criticize the ideas of others.

2. The chairman sees that people do not all speak at once. (The chairman must also pick out someone who has been trying to say

something but is always outspoken by a more pushy character.) The chairman *does not* have to ask individuals to speak. They speak when they want to. Nor does he go round the circle asking each in turn for ideas. If however there is a prolonged silence the chairman may ask an individual for his thoughts on the matter.

3. The chairman sees that the notetaker has got an idea down. The chairman may find it necessary to repeat an idea or even to summarize an idea offered by a participant (this summary must be approved by the person whose idea it was.) The chairman may be asked to decide whether an idea is already on the list and so does not need listing again. If there is any doubt or the originator of the idea claims it to be different then it must be listed.

4. The chairman fills in gaps by offering suggestions himself. He may also call on the notetaker to read through the list of ideas already recorded.

5. The chairman can suggest different ways of tackling the problem and the use of different lateral thinking techniques for trying to generate different ways of looking at the problem (e.g. the chairman may say, 'Let's try turning this thing upside down.') Anyone else may of course make the same suggestions.

6. The chairman defines the central problem and keeps pulling people back to it. This is a difficult task since apparently irrelevant flights of fancy may be very generative and one certainly does not want to restrict people to the obvious view of the problem. As a guiding rule it may be said that any single flight of fancy is allowed but sustained divergence so that one comes to be considering a totally different problem is not allowed.

7. The chairman ends the session either at the end of a set time or if the session seems to be flagging – whichever is earlier. The chairman must not run the risk of boring people by extending the session indefinitely if it seems to be going well.

8. The chairman organizes the evaluation session and the listing of ideas.

● Notetaker

The function of the notetaker is to convert into a permanent list the many butterfly ideas that are put forward during the session.

The task is a difficult one since the nebulous ideas offered must be reduced to manageable note form. Moreover the notes must not only make sense immediately after the session but some time later when the context is no longer so clear. The notetaker has to write fast for sometimes the ideas follow one another very rapidly. The notetaker can ask the chairman to hold things until he can catch up. The notetaker may also ask whether a particular summary of the idea is acceptable (e.g. shall we put this down as, 'More flexible traffic light system'?).

The notetaker must also assess whether an idea is new enough to be added to the list or whether it is already covered by a similar idea. If in doubt he should ask the chairman. It is better to put down duplicate ideas than leave out different ones, for the duplicate ones can be removed later but the omitted ones are lost forever.

The notes must be in a form that is immediately readable, for the chairman may ask for the list to be read out at any stage. It is not a matter of carefully transcribing shorthand some time after the end of the session.

It is useful to tape record a session as the playback may set off new ideas by repeating early ideas in a new context. Nevertheless even when the session is so recorded it is still essential to have a notetaker. At some time a summary list has to be made even of a tape and there is also the need to read out the list during the session.

● Time

Thirty minutes is quite long enough for a session. Twenty minutes would be enough in many cases and forty-five minutes is an outside limit. It is better to stop while people are still full of ideas than to carry on until every last idea has been forced out. The temptation to carry on if the session is going well must be resisted.

● Warm up

If the members of the group are not familiar with the technique (and perhaps even if they are) a ten minute warm up session is useful. This would deal with some very simple problem (bathtap design, bus tickets, telephone bells). The idea of this warm up session is to show the type of ideas that may be offered and to show that evaluation is excluded.

● Follow up

After the main session is over the participants will continue to have ideas on the subject. These can be collected by asking each participant to send in a list of further ideas. If copying facilities are available then the list of ideas generated during the session can be sent to each participant with instructions to add any further ideas of his own on the bottom.

Evaluation

As indicated above there is no attempt at evaluation during the brainstorming session itself. Any tendency to evaluate would kill spontaneity and convert the session into one of critical analysis. Evaluation is carried out later by the same group or even by another group. It is important that some sort of evaluation is carried out even if the problem is not a real one. It is the evaluation session that makes a worthwhile activity of what would otherwise be a frivolous exercise. In the evaluation session the list of ideas is sifted to extract the useful ore. The main points in the evaluation are as follows:

1. To pick out ideas which are directly useful.
2. To extract from ideas that are wrong or ridiculous the functional kernel of the idea which may be generalized in a useful way (e.g. in a brainstorming session considering the problem of rail transport one idea put forward was that trains should have tracks on their roofs so that when two trains met one could pass above the other. The functional idea here is fuller utilization of the same track or better use of carriage roofs.) The idea of using a magnet to pull apples from the trees would be considered as

finding a means to bring apples *en masse* to the ground instead of picking them individually or as pretreatment of the apples in order to make them easy to pick.

3. To list functional ideas, new aspects of the problem, ways of considering the problem, additional factors to be taken into consideration. None of these are actual solutions to the problem but merely approaches.

4. To pick out those ideas which can be tried out with relative ease even though they may seem wrong at first sight.

5. To pick out those ideas which suggest that more information could be collected in certain areas.

 • 6. To pick out those ideas which have in fact already been tried out.

At the end of the evaluation session there should be three lists:
● Ideas of immediate usefulness.
● Areas for further exploration.
● New approaches to the problem.

The evaluation session is not just a mechanical sorting, for some creative effort is required to extract usefulness from ideas before they are discarded or to spot an idea which looks as if it ought to be discarded but can in fact be developed into something significant.

Formulation of the problem

While any problem can be the subject of a brainstorming session the way the problem is formulated can make a huge difference to the success with which it is tackled.

Too wide a statement of the problem may bring about a variety of ideas but they are so separated that they cannot interact to bring about that chain reaction of stimulation that is the basis of brainstorming. The statement of a problem as, 'Better traffic control', would be too wide.

Too narrow a statement of the problem restricts ideas so much that the session may end up generating ideas not about the problem itself but about some particular way of handling it. The statement of a problem as, 'To improve traffic lights', would not lead to ideas about traffic control by means other than traffic lights. It might not even lead to ideas on better traffic control by traffic lights for attention might focus on ease of manufacture, ease of maintenance and reliability of traffic lights quite apart from their functional importance.

It is the chairman's duty to state the problem at the beginning of the session and to repeat this statement frequently in the course of the session. If it should prove to have been stated badly then he – or anyone else in the group – can suggest a better way of stating it. A suitable statement of the problem mentioned above would be: 'Methods of improving traffic flow given the present arrangement of roads.'

Examples

Transcript 1

The following is a transcription of part of a brainstorming session that was considering the redesign of a teaspoon.

... A rubber spoon.

... I feel that the secondary function of a spoon which is that of transferring sugar from the basin to the cup has largely disappeared and that a teaspoon in the shape of an egg whisk would be much more efficient.

... (Put down egg whisk.)

... And make it electrically driven.

... Incorporate a musical box for the aesthetic function.

... Have something like a pipette tube which you dip in the sugar with your finger over the top and transfer sugar in that way. Then the sugar would be provided with a dispersing agent so that you would entirely lose the pleasure of stirring.

... Going back to the egg whisk I think one ought to have a sort of screw thing, rather like an electrical swizzle stick. The axle would be hollow ...

... (Can I interrupt here? You are beginning to tell us how you would make it and that is not the function of this session.)

... No, I am just describing what it looks like.

... (Could you describe it more simply?)

... A rotating spoon?

... No, it's got a screw. You know, a propeller type screw.

... You push it up and down?

... No, it's electric, you just press the button on the top.

... It seems to me this is too complicated. Now you have ordinary sugar tongs and each individual would have his own sugar tongs and would pick up a couple of lumps of sugar. The tongs have two ends and you could create turbulence just as easily as with a spoon.

... Doesn't this restrict you to lump sugar?

... Yes, small lumps. But you can still get the quantity of sugar you want.

... (What shall we put down there?)

... Tongs.

... What about something like those ashtrays which spin as you press them. We could have something that you placed over a cup and as you pressed it it opened out to release some sugar and at the same time spun to stir the sugar in.

... If there is so much fun stirring in sugar then perhaps we ought to have some sort of inert sugar which people who don't like sugar could use in order to enjoy stirring in.

... A once off spoon made of sugar.

... A device which contains sugar and which is moved up and down in the cup. But if you don't want sugar you keep a gate closed.

... I would like to take up the idea of electricity but not using a battery or anything like that but using the static electricity present in the body.

... This idea of a screw. One could do it on the autogiro principle. As the screw went up and down the fluid would make it revolve.

... Like a spinning top.

... A vibrating table that would agitate everything on it – whether you had sugar or not.

... What about a sugar impregnated stick.

Transcript 2

The session was attempting to discover a better design for the windscreen wiper/washer function. Something to prevent impairment of vision by an accumulation of mud and/or water.

... A conventional windscreen wiper with water or some other washing agent coming in through the arms of the wiper itself instead of being sprayed onto the screen from another point.

... A rotating centrifugal disc...

... Like on a ship?

... Yes.

... How about doing away with the screen and just having a very fast flow of air through which no particles of dust or water could penetrate?

... A wiper that would move straight across the screen from side to side or from top to bottom, the rate to be controlled by the driver.

... Have a liquid which makes the dirt transparent so you don't have to take it off.

... A screen that acts as a shutter and wipes itself clean as it revolves.

... An electrically heated screen that boils off the water.

... Radar control of the car itself.

... A high speed screen that ejected some liquid as it went up and wiped it off as it came down.

... Ultrasonics.

... Make mudflaps compulsory on all vehicles.

... Develop two types of magnet, one of which attracts water and the other attracts dirt and locate them on the bottom.

... Channel water off the roof of the cab and so make wipers less necessary.

... Have a liquid windscreen.

... How about a surface which is perpetually in motion?

... Vibration.

... Have a circular car with a windscreen that passes round it and through a washer on the way round.

... Windscreen wiper with jets in the wiper.

... (I think we have that down already as jets in the wiper arm itself.)

... Experiment with rotating sponges and brushes and things other than the conventional sweeper.

... Sheet of water flowing down the windscreen and get rid of the wipers altogether.

... (So far we have been trying to get rid of the wiper. Suppose we did not want to get rid of the wiper but just to improve it. Is there any way we could do things hydraulically?)

... A very high pressure jet of water that would dislodge the dirt and also provide volume for washing it away.

... Experiment with partial windscreen so that you don't actually look through glass, you look through a gap.

... 3, 6 or 8 or any number of wipers operating along the bottom or along the top and sides of the screen.

... Have two fairly conventional windscreens that go up and down alternately and pass through wipers as they go up and down.

... Have a rotating screen, part of which went underneath where it was cleaned so you always had a fresh piece.

... Have a choice of washer tanks so you could vary the liquid according to the conditions – for instance using something special to wash off oil.

... A periscope that you could see above the dirt.

... Have a venetian blind principle.

... Have a double thickness of glass with water in between. The front sheet would have small holes through which the water was constantly trickling.

... Some screen that would intercept most of the dirt before it reached the windscreen proper.

... Change the driving position. Turn around and drive from the back.

... Drive in tunnels.

... Television arrangement so that the driver does not have to actually look out.

... An ordinary wiper with a variable speed which is automatically adjusted according to the speed of the car or the amount of light getting through the windscreen or something like that.

... Have a multi-layer windscreen in which you just peel off the outer dirty layer.

... Have a soluble surface windscreen so that the water is constantly dissolving it and so keeping it clean.

... Have windscreen made of ice which is constantly melting and so keeping itself clean.

... You could just put a layer of the soluble stuff on before you went out.

Comment

The remarks within brackets were made by the chairman. No attempt is made to distinguish the remarks of the other participants. The nature of the suggestions varies from the outright ridiculous to the solid and sensible. It may also be seen how one idea springs from another. There is very little attempt at evaluation. Almost every remark contributes a new idea.

Practice

The classroom is divided up into groups of a suitable size for a brainstorming session. Each group elects its own chairman. If there is any difficulty about this then the teacher makes a suggestion. The notetaker is also selected in each group. It may be useful to have an auxiliary notetaker who can relieve the first one halfway through the session.

The general principles of the brainstorming session are explained with emphasis on the following points:

1. No criticism or evaluation.
2. Say anything you like no matter how wrong or ridiculous.
3. Do not try and develop ideas at length or make speeches, a few words are enough.
4. Give the notetaker a chance to get things down.
5. Listen to the chairman.

A warm up problem is then given to each group and they have a ten minute warm up session. At the end of this session they go straight into the main session for thirty minutes.

The teacher may sit in on the groups in turn. It is better not to be too intrusive. Few comments are made at the time but mental notes are kept for discussion afterwards. The only thing which justifies an intervention is any tendency to evaluate or criticize.

At the end of the sessions the groups come together again. In turn the notetakers from each group read out the list of ideas. The teacher may then comment as follows:

1. Comments on the actual session stressing perhaps the tendency to evaluate or the tendency to be too timid.

2. Comments on the lists of ideas. These could point out the similarity of some of the ideas, the originality of others.

3. Comments on the tone of the ideas. Some of the suggestions may have been quite sensible others quite ridiculous. If the suggestions do tend to be too solemn the teacher might point out that at least some of the suggestions during the sessions should be outrageous enough to cause a laugh.

4. The teacher then adds some ideas and suggestions of his own concerning the problems that have been discussed.

In going through the lists of suggestions the teacher may pick out some of the more outrageous ideas and proceed to show how they can be useful. This is done by extracting the functional principle of the idea and developing it further.

The general impression that should be encouraged is that the brainstorming session is a generative situation in which one should not be too selfconscious. In practice there is a tendency for some students to show off and try to be deliberately humorous if they know that their suggestions are to be read out to the assembled class. One has to deal with that situation as best one can without denying people the right to be outrageous. One way is to ask the person to explain the idea further.

Suggested problems for use in brainstorming sessions might include:

The design of money.
The lack of sufficient playgrounds.
The need for examinations.
Mining under the sea.

Providing enough television programmes for everyone to see what they want to see.
Making the desert fertile.
Heating a house.

In each case what is being asked for is a way of doing it, a better way of doing it, a new way of doing it. These are merely suggestions and the teacher ought to be able to generate further problems.

● Evaluation

Evaluation sessions should not be held on the same day as the brainstorming sessions. The evaluation sessions are best done in front of the whole class and each idea is considered in turn for its direct or indirect usefulness.

One can have different categories into which each idea is placed. These might be:
Directly useful.
Interesting approach.
For further examination.
Discard.

An alternative to this general evaluation is to write the brainstorm lists on the blackboard a few items at a time and get each student to evaluate the items with votes. At the end the different evaluations can be compared by seeing how many 'votes' each item gets.

In this context the evaluation session is a necessary part of the brainstorm session but not an important part. Evaluations tend to be critical analysis and vertical thinking. Emphasis should be directed much more to the brainstorm session itself than to the subsequent evaluation.

It is important in any attempt at evaluation not to give the impression that the outrageous ideas were only of use in the brainstorming session but not of much practical use anywhere else. Such an impression would limit suggestions to the practical and the solemnly sensible which though worthwhile in themselves would never lead to new ideas. One of the most important functions of the evaluation session is to show that even the most outrageous suggestions can lead to useful ideas.

Summary

The brainstorming session is of value as a formal setting which encourages the use of lateral thinking. The brainstorming session has a value as a group activity in which there is a cross stimulation of ideas. Otherwise there is nothing special to a brainstorming session that could not be done outside it. Some people equate creative thinking with brainstorming. This is to equate a basic process with one relatively minor setting which encourages the use of that process. Perhaps the most important part of the brainstorming session is its formality. When one is first getting used to the idea of lateral thinking it is helpful to have some special setting in which to practise it. Later on there is less need for such a setting.

In order to restructure a pattern, to look at a situation in a different way, to have new ideas, one must start having some ideas. The two problems of lateral thinking are:

● To get going, to get some movement, to start a train of thought.

● To escape the natural, obvious, cliché train of thought.

The various techniques described so far have all been concerned with generating some movement. So is the analogy technique.

In itself an analogy is a simple story or situation. It becomes an analogy only when it is compared to something else. The simple story or situation must be familiar. Its line of development must be familiar. There must be something happening or some process going on or some special type of relationship to observe. There must be some development either in the situation itself or at least in the way it is looked at. Boiling an egg is a simple operation, but there is development in it. The egg is placed in a special container and heated. In order to bring the heat into better contact with the egg a liquid is used. This liquid also serves to prevent the temperature from rising above a certain value. In the process the egg changes its nature. This change is a progressive one that is proportional to the amount of time the egg remains in this special situation. Different people have sharply different tastes about how far they want the process to go.

The important point about an analogy is that it has a 'life' of its own. This 'life' can be expressed directly in terms of the actual objects involved or it can be expressed in terms of the processes involved. One can talk of putting an egg into water in a saucepan and boiling it for four minutes until the white is hard but the yolk still quite runny. Or one can talk of the changing state of an object with time when that object is subjected to certain circumstances. Analogies are vehicles for relationships and processes. These relationships and processes are embodied in actual objects such as boiled eggs but the relationship and processes can be generalized to other situations.

The analogy does not have to be complicated or long. A simple activity may suffice. Butterfly collecting is a special hobby yet the processes involved can be generalized to many other situations (e.g. rarity, supply and demand; information and search procedures; beauty and rarity; interference with nature for one's own uses; classification).

Analogies are used to provide movement. The problem under consideration is related to the analogy and then the analogy is developed along its own lines of development. At each stage the development is transferred back to the original problem. Thus the problem is carried along with the analogy. In mathematics one translates things into symbols and then deals with these symbols by means of various mathematical operations. One forgets all about the real meaning of the symbols. At the end the symbols are translated back and one finds out what has become of the original situation. The mathematical operation is a channel which directs the development of the original problem.

Analogies can be used in the same way. One can translate the problem into an analogy and then develop the analogy. At the end one translates back and sees what might have happened to the original problem. It is probably more useful to develop the two in parallel. What is happening in the analogy is transferred (as a process or relationship) to the actual problem.

For instance one might use the analogy of a snowball rolling down a hill to investigate the spread of rumours. As the snowball rolls down the hill the farther it goes the bigger it gets. (The more a rumour spreads the stronger it gets.) As the snowball gets bigger it picks up more and more new snow. (The more people who know the rumour the more people it gets passed onto.) But for the snowball to increase in size there must be snow. At this point one is not sure whether the size of the snowball is being compared to the number of people who know the rumour or the strength of the rumour. Does the snow on the ground correspond merely to people who can be influenced by the rumour or to people predisposed to believe this sort of rumour? One is already being forced by the analogy to look hard at the problem itself. A large snowball – perhaps an avalanche – can be very destructive but if one is forewarned one can get out of the way. (A rumour can also be destructive but can one get out of the way if fore-warned, should one try to escape, to stop it, or to divert it?)

Using an analogy in this way is very different from arguing by analogy. In argument by analogy one supposes that because some-thing happens in a certain way in the analogy then it must happen in the same way in the problem situation. The use of analogies in lateral thinking is completely different. As usual one is not trying to prove anything. Analogies are used as a method for generating further ideas.

Choosing an analogy

It might be thought that the method would only be of use if a particularly apt analogy were chosen. This is not so. The analogy does not have to fit all along. Sometimes it is better when it does not fit for then there is an effort to relate it to the problem and from this effort can arise new ways of looking at the problem. The analogy is a provocative device which is used to force a new way of looking at the situation.

In general the analogies should deal with very concrete situa-tions and very familiar ones. There should be a lot going on. And what is going on must be definite. The analogy does not have to be rich in processes or functions or relationships for these can be generated out of any sort of analogy by the way it is looked at.

The analogy does not even have to be a real life situation. It can be a story provided the development of that story is definite.

As an analogy for the problem of vertical thinking one might use the story of how monkeys are supposedly caught by burying a narrow mouthed jar of nuts in the ground. A monkey comes along, puts his paw into the jar and grabs a handful of nuts. But the mouth of the jar is of such a size that it will only admit an empty paw but not a clenched paw full of nuts. The monkey is unwilling to let go of the nuts and so he is trapped.

With vertical thinking one grasps the obvious way of looking at a situation because it has proved useful in the past. Once one has grasped it one is trapped because one is very reluctant to let go. What should the monkey do? Should he refuse to explore the jar? This would be a refusal to explore new situations. Should he deny that the nuts were attractive? It would be silly to deny the usefulness of something for fear of being harmed by it on some occasion. Would it be better if the monkey had not noticed the jar? To be protected by chance is a very poor form of protection. Presumably the best thing would be for the monkey to see the nuts, perhaps even grab them, then to realize that the nuts were trapping it, to let go of them, and to find another way of getting at the nuts – perhaps by digging up the jar and emptying it out. So the major danger in vertical thinking is not that of being trapped by the obvious but of failing to realize that one may be trapped by the obvious. It is not a matter of avoiding vertical thinking but of using it and at the same time being aware that it might be necessary to escape from a particular way of looking at a situation.

Practice

1. Demonstration
In order to make clear what is wanted during the practice sessions, it is useful to start by taking a particular problem, choosing an analogy, developing the analogy and relating it to the problem all along. This could be done on the blackboard. Suggestions from students would be accepted but they would not be asked for.

2. Relating an analogy to the problem
The problem would be given to the class. The teacher would

develop an analogy on the blackboard and the students would be asked to volunteer at each point a suggestion as to how any particular development in the analogy could be referred to the given problem.

3. Individual effort

Here the analogy would again be developed by the teacher but this time the individual students would each relate it to the problem, writing down their ideas on a piece of paper. At the end these results would be collected and comments of the following sort could be made:

(1). The variety of different ways in which the analogy was related to the problem.

(2). Consistency or lack of consistency in the development of the problem (i.e. was a feature in the analogy always referred to the same feature in the problem or did it change? There is no special virtue in consistency.)

(3). Richness of development with every detail translated from the analogy to the problem or poverty of development when only the major points were transferred.

4. Functions, processes, relationships

Here an analogy is developed by the teacher in concrete terms. The students (working on their own) have to repeat the analogy but using general terms of process, function and relationship, in place of the concrete terms. This is an exercise in *abstracting* these things from analogies.

Possible analogies for this sort of abstraction might include:
Having a bath.
Frying potatoes.
Sending a letter.
Trying to untangle a ball of string.
Learning to swim.

5. Choosing analogies

A list of problems or situations would be given to the students who would be asked in open class to volunteer analogies which might be fitted to each of the listed problems. Any student who volunteered a suggestion would be asked to elaborate it briefly by showing how he would apply it to the problem.

Possible problems for this exercise might include:

Design a machine to give change.
Ways of making shopping easier.
Better clothes.
Ensuring adequate water supply for cities.
What to do with junked cars.

6. Set problem

A problem is given to the classroom and each student chooses his own analogy and works through it relating it to the problem. At the end the results are collected and commented upon. In the course of such comments one might compare the different types of analogy chosen. One might also compare the different aspects of the problem that have been highlighted by the different analogies. There may be occasions when the same idea has been reached by completely different pathways.

7. Same problem, different analogies

The same problem is given to all the students but different students are assigned different analogies. This can be done as a group exercise. The students are divided into groups all of which are to consider the same problem. Each group however is given a different analogy. At the end of the session a spokesman for the group (equivalent to the notetaker in the brainstorming session) summarizes how the group related the analogy to the problem.

Suggested problem:
Finding the way in fog.

Suggested analogies:
A shortsighted person finding his way around.
A traveller in a strange country trying to find the railway station.
Looking for something that has been lost in the house (e.g. a ball of string).
Doing a crossword puzzle.

8. Same analogy, different problems

This can be carried out in the same way as the previous session, either on an individual basis or on a group basis. Different problems are set but in each case they must be related to the same analogy. At the end notes are compared to see how well the analogy has been fitted to the different problems.

Suggested analogy:
Trying to start a car on a cold winter morning.

Suggested problems:
How to tackle a difficult mathematical problem.
Rescuing a cat from a high ledge.
Fishing.
Getting tickets for a very popular football match.

Summary

Analogies offer a convenient method for getting going when one is trying to find new ways of looking at a situation instead of just waiting for inspiration. As with other lateral thinking techniques the important point is that one does not start moving only when one can see where one is going. One starts moving for the sake of moving and then sees what happens. An analogy is a convenient way of getting moving for analogies have a definite 'life' of their own. There is no attempt to use analogies to prove anything. They are only used as stimulation. The main usefulness of analogies is as vehicles for functions, processes, and relationships, which can then be transferred to the problem under consideration to help restructure it.

The most important feature of the mind as an information processing system is its ability to choose. This ability to choose arises directly from the mechanical behaviour of the mind as a self-maximizing memory system. Such a system has a limited area of attention. A limited area of attention can only settle on part of an information field. That part of the information field on which the limited attention area settles is thereby 'chosen' or 'selected'. The process is in fact a passive one but one can still talk of choice or selection. The behaviour of this limited attention area and the system mechanics underlying it are explained in detail elsewhere.*

'Attention area' refers to the part of a situation or problem that is attended to. 'Entry point' refers to the part of a problem or situation that is *first* attended to. An entry point is obviously the first area of attention and it may or may not be succeeded by others depending on the complexity of the situation.

From an insight restructuring point of view the choice of entry point is of the utmost importance. One could almost say that when no further information is added to the system that it is the choice of entry point which brings about insight restructuring. Why this is so follows directly from the mechanics of this type of information processing system.*

Patterns are established on the memory surface that is mind by the sequence of arrival of information. Once established these patterns have a 'natural' behaviour in so far as they tend to develop in certain ways, and to link up with other patterns. The purpose of lateral thinking is to restructure these patterns and arrange information to give new patterns.

1 field

2 pattern

3 development

4 entry point

5 other pattern

The series of diagrams above illustrates the natural patterning behaviour of the memory surface of mind:

1. This shows the available information field.

2. Information is structured into a natural pattern.

3. The natural pattern has a natural line of development.

4. In developing the pattern there is a natural entry point from which one starts.

5. From the original information field only a limited area was selected by attention. Had the attention field been different then the pattern and its development would also have been different.

The choice of entry point is of huge importance because the historical sequence in which ideas follow one another can completely determine the final outcome even if the ideas themselves are the same. If you fill a bath using only the hot tap and then add the cold water at the end the bathroom will be thoroughly steamed up and the walls will be damp. If however you run some of the cold water in right at the beginning then there will be no steaming up and the walls will remain dry. Yet the actual amounts of hot and cold water will be exactly the same in each case.

The difference may be huge even if the actual ideas considered are the same but in practice a different entry point will usually mean a different train of ideas. A picture of a man with a stick in his hand followed by a picture of a dog running might suggest that the man is throwing sticks for the dog to retrieve. A picture of a dog running followed by a picture of the man with a stick in his hand might suggest that the man is chasing the dog out of his garden.

Entry point

Divide a triangle into three parts in such a way that the parts can be put together again to form a rectangle or a square.

The problem is quite a difficult one since the shape of the triangle is not specified. You first have to choose a triangle shape and then find out how it can be divided up into three pieces that can be put together to give the square or rectangle.

The solution to the problem is shown opposite. It is obviously much easier to start with the square instead of with the triangle which was suggested as the starting point. There can be no doubt about the shape of a square whereas the shape of a triangle (and to a lesser extent of a rectangle) is variable. Since the three parts have to fit together again to form a square one can solve the problem by dividing up a square into three parts that can be put together again to give a rectangle or a triangle. Two ways of doing this are shown overleaf.

In many children's books there is the sort of puzzle in which are shown three fishermen whose lines have got tangled up. At the bottom of the picture a fish is shown attached to one of the lines. The problem is to find which fisherman has caught the fish. The children are supposed to follow the line down from the tip of the fishing rod in order to find which line has the fish at the end. This may involve one, two or three attempts since the fish may be on any of the three lines. It is obviously much easier to start at the other end and trace the line upwards from the fish to the fisherman. That way there need never be more than one attempt.

There is a simple problem which requires one to draw the outline of a piece of cardboard which is so shaped that with a single straight cut the piece can be divided into four smaller pieces which are exactly alike in size, shape and area. No folding is allowed.

The usual response to this problem is shown on page 159 with the percentage of people giving each type of answer. The solution given by groups B and C is obviously incorrect for a 'cut' has no thickness and so will divide the shape into two pieces and not four as required.

Answer D is correct. It is interesting that answer F is so rare for in hindsight it seems the easiest of them all (the explanation is that it is very difficult to think forward asymmetrically and in answer F the pieces are not all used in the same way). The important point of this problem, however, is that if one starts at the wrong end the problem is much easier to solve. Instead of trying to devise a shape that can be divided into four equal pieces one starts off with four equal pieces and clusters them around an imaginary cut. At first one might arrange them as shown on page 160 but there is no difficulty in moving on to the next stage in which one shifts them along to give the solution.

To start at the wrong end and work backwards is quite a well-known problem solving technique. The reason why it is effective is that the line of thought may be quite different from what it would have been had one started at the beginning. There is no

35% A impossible

50% B   or C

12% D   or E

3% F

need to actually start at the solution end. It is convenient to do so since the solution is often clearly defined. But one can start at any point. If there is no obvious point then one must be generated.

Attention area

The entry point is the first attention area. Usually attention starts at this point but eventually covers the whole problem. Sometimes however important parts of the problem are completely left out. It is only when these parts are brought under attention that the problem can be solved.

In one of Sherlock Holmes's cases there was a large dog. Dr Watson dismissed the dog as being of no importance because it had done nothing on the night of the crime. Sherlock Holmes pointed out that the great significance of the dog was precisely that it had done nothing. He shifted attention from the significance of what the dog might have done to the significance of the fact that it had done nothing. This meant that the criminal must have been known to the dog.

In Shakespeare's *Merchant of Venice* there comes the moment when Shylock demands the pound of flesh that is owed to him by the merchant as the result of a bargain. Shylock is outwitted by Portia who shifts attention from the flesh which is due to Shylock to the blood that must go with it. Since that is not part of the bargain Shylock could be charged with the serious offence of spilling blood. Thus by a shift of attention which brought into the problem something that would otherwise have been left out the problem was solved.

Two sets of circles are shown overleaf. In each case count up the number of solid circles as quickly as possible.

The obvious way to tackle this problem is to count the solid circles in each case. But when you come to the second set of circles it is much easier to shift attention to the open circles, find out the total number of these by multiplying the number of circles along one edge of the rectangle by the number along the other edge, and then subtract the small number of open circles from this total. The answer is the number of filled circles.

In a tennis tournament there are one hundred and eleven entrants. It is a singles knockout tournament and you as secretary have to arrange the matches. What is the minimum number of matches that would have to be arranged with this number of entrants?

When faced with this problem most people draw little diagrams showing the actual pairings in each match and the number of byes. Others try and work it out by reference to 2^n (i.e. 4, 8, 16, 32 etc). In fact the answer is one hundred and ten matches and one can work this out at once without any complicated mathematics. To work it out one must shift attention from the winners of each match to the losers (in whom no one is usually very interested). Since there can only be one winner there must be one hundred and ten losers. Each loser can only lose once so there must be one hundred and ten matches.

In a sense this last problem could be regarded as an example of the usefulness of shifting the entry point except that the losers are usually never considered at all. Very often in a situation it is not just a matter of the order in which the parts are attended to but the choice of parts that are going to be attended to at all. If something is left out of consideration then it is very unlikely that it will ever come back in later on. Nor is there usually anything in what is being attended to that will indicate what has been left out.

For these reasons the choice of attention area can make a huge difference to the way the situation is looked at. To restructure the situation one may need no more than a slight shift in attention. On the other hand if there is no shift in attention it may be very difficult to look at the situation in a different way.

Rotation of attention

Since attention is basically a passive phenomenon it is no use just hoping that attention will flow in the right direction. One has to do something about it. Even though the process is passive one can still direct attention by providing a framework which will affect it. For instance you could decide that whenever you found yourself staring at something then you would shift your gaze to a spot about two feet to the left of whatever you were staring at. After a while attention would automatically shift to that spot even though there was nothing there which attracted it. Attention follows the patterns set up in the mind not the external ones.

As with the reversal procedure one can deliberately turn away from what one would naturally pay attention to in order to see what happens if one paid attention to something else. For instance in the tennis tournament problem one might have said, 'I am trying to see how many matches there would have to be to produce one winner – instead of this let me see how many matches there would have to be to produce 110 losers.' This reversal procedure can work very well if there is a definite natural focus of attention in the situation.

Another method is to list the different features of the situation and then to proceed methodically through this list paying attention to each feature in turn. The important point here is not to feel that some features are so trivial that they do not merit any attention. The difficulty is that in any situation one can pick out as many features as one likes since the features reside not in the situation but in the way it is looked at.

Suppose one was considering the problem of homework. One might list the following features for attention in rotation:
Necessity for doing it (optional or required).
Time in which to do it.
Essential to course or reinforcing.
Travel time to get home.
Place to do it at home.
What else might be done instead.
Competing television programmes.
Routine or occasional.
Ability of father or mother to help.
Fast workers and slow workers.
Is one interested in what is done or the amount of time spent doing it?
Frustration and annoyance of homework.
Homework as lessening the content or impact of schoolwork.

Suppose the problem was one of getting rid of weeds. The natural attention focus is the growth of weeds which leads to methods for getting rid of them. But no attention is paid to what happens after the weeds are gone or to what would happen if the weeds were to stay. Attention is on the weeds and getting rid of them. In a recent experiment some strips in a field were sprayed with the usual weedkiller and others left to grow weeds. It was found that the yield of crops from the unsprayed strips was in fact higher.

In a foot and mouth epidemic it is customary to burn the corpses of infected animals if the soil is not deep enough to bury them. But in the burning, currents of hot air rise and spread particles from the fire over a very wide area. It is possible that such particles might be infected with virus that has escaped the full heat of the fire and so the disease might tend to spread. Here the attention is on getting rid of the infected animals not on the effect of the method used for getting rid of them.

A very useful drug in medicine was discovered when someone noticed that when the drug was being used for something quite different the patients always passed a lot of urine. Since this was not the purpose of the treatment no one paid any attention to it until someone suddenly realized that here was a useful drug which could make patients pass urine when this *was* the purpose of treatment.

Practice

1. Identify entry points

An article discussing a particular problem is read out or given to the students. They are asked to list possible entry points for tackling the problem. They are also asked to define the entry point used by the writer of the article. For instance in an article on world hunger the writer might have chosen the wastage of food in some countries as his entry point, or he might have chosen overpopulation or inefficient agriculture. From the results the teacher lists the possible entry points that have been suggested and adds other ones.

2. Entry points for assorted problems

A list of problems is written up on the blackboard and the students are asked in open class to volunteer different entry points for each of the problems. Each student offering a suggestion is asked to elaborate it briefly.

Possible problems might include:

The making of synthetic foods.

The acceptance of synthetic foods.

A better design for a sausage.

The problem of stray dogs.

An easy method for cleaning windows.

3. Same problem, different entry points

This could be done by individuals or as a group activity. The same problem is set for all the groups but each group is given a different entry point. At the end a spokesman for each group discusses how they used the entry point in each group. The point to watch here is that the group really does use the entry point. There is a temptation to consider the problem in the obvious way and then just to connect up the entry point with this obvious way.

Suggested problem:

A method for keeping rain off one while one is walking in the street.

Suggested points of entry:

Bother of having to carry an umbrella.
Awkwardness of umbrellas when several people are using them.
Why go out in the rain?
Why does getting wet matter?

4. Omitted information (story)

In telling a story one normally leaves out all the information which is not essential for the development of the story. But if one wants to examine the situation itself rather than the way it has been described by someone else then one has to try and put that information back. One takes a story which may come from a newspaper or may be a very well-known story. In open class the students are asked for suggestions as to what has been left out.

e.g. Jack and Jill went up the hill to fetch a pail of water. Jack fell down and broke his crown and Jill came tumbling after.

Was it on the way up or on the way back?
Was Jill hurt?
Why did Jill fall down anyway?
Why did Jack fall down?
Why were they going uphill to collect water?

5. Omitted information (picture)

Here a photograph or picture is used instead of a story. One student examines the picture and describes it to the classroom. Then each of the students draws a simple version of what he thinks the described picture looks like. From the nature of these drawings one can see the information that was omitted in the description of the picture. Another way of doing it is for a student to describe the picture as before and for the rest of the students to ask questions. Whenever a question can be answered from the picture then the student describing it could not have been paying attention to that part of the picture.

6. Further information

A picture is shown to the whole classroom. Each student writes down the information that he can get from that picture. At the end the results are collected and compared. The comparison between the person who extracts the *most* information and the person who extracts the *least* demonstrates how limited an area of attention may be.

7. Checklist

A problem is given and the students are asked to list all the different features through which they would like to rotate attention. This can be done in open class on a volunteer basis or by individual students with comparison of the lists at the end.

Suggested problems might include :

Alarm clocks that fail to wake one up.

Design for a bathtub.

Putting up a washing line.

Deciding where to build an airport.

Reducing noise from motorcycles and lorries.

8. Detective stories

With most detective stories there is difficulty in finding the criminal because certain factors are left out of consideration or the wrong entry point is chosen. The writer of a good detective story tries to bring about both these mistakes. The teacher devises a short detective story which contains enough clues to indicate who the criminal might be. The story is then read out to the class who each have to decide for themselves who the criminal is and why. The students should then be asked to write their own detective stories on these lines. These stories in turn are read out to the class. For each story there is an assessment of how many students reach the right conclusion. The author of the story may be called upon to show how he has included enough clues to indicate the criminal.

Summary

Because of the nature of the self-maximizing memory system of the mind the entry point for considering a situation or a problem can make a big difference to the way it is structured. Usually the obvious entry point is chosen. Such an entry point is itself determined by the established pattern and so leads back to this. There is no way of telling which entry point is going to be best so one is usually content with the most obvious one. It is assumed that the choice of entry point does not matter since one will always arrive at the same conclusions. This is not so since the whole train of thought may be determined by the choice of entry point. It is useful to develop some skill in picking out and following different entry points.

The attention area is limited and includes much less information than is available. If something is left out of consideration then there is nothing which will make it come back into consideration at a later point. What is there does not usually indicate what is missing. Attention usually settles over the most obvious areas. A slight shift in attention may by itself restructure a situation. One tries deliberately to rotate attention over all parts of the problem, especially those which do not seem to merit it.

The three ways of encouraging lateral thinking discussed in this book are:
● Awareness of the principles of lateral thinking, the need for lateral thinking, the rigidity of vertical thinking patterns.
● The use of some definite technique which develops the original pattern and may bring about restructuring.
● The deliberate alteration of circumstances so that they can stimulate restructuring.

Most of the techniques discussed so far have worked from within the idea. The idea has been developed according to some routine process with the intention of allowing the information to snap together again in a new pattern. But instead of trying to work from within the idea one can deliberately generate external stimulation which then acts on the idea from outside. This is how random stimulation works.

Some of the lateral methods discussed in this book have not been very different from vertical methods though the way they were used and the intention behind them may have been different. The use of random stimulation is fundamentally different from vertical thinking. With vertical thinking one deals only with what is relevant. In fact one spends most of one's time selecting out what is relevant and what is not. With random stimulation one uses any information whatsoever. No matter how unrelated it may be no information is rejected as useless. The more irrelevant the information the more useful it may be.

Generating random inputs

The two main ways of bringing about random stimulation are:

● Exposure.

● Formal generation.

Exposure

The division between exposure and formal generation of random stimulation is only one of convenience. If one actively puts oneself into a position where one is subjected to random stimulation that is part exposure and part formal generation. The following points may serve to illustrate the way random stimulation can be used.

    1. Accepting and even welcoming random inputs. Instead of shutting out something which does not appear relevant one regards it as a random input and pays it attention. This involves no further activity than an attitude that notices what comes along.

    2. Exposure to the ideas of others. In a brainstorming session the ideas of others act as random inputs in the sense that they do not have to follow one's own line of thought even though they occupy the same field of relevance. Listening to others even if one disagrees very strongly with their ideas can provide useful input.

    3. Exposure to ideas from completely different fields. This sometimes goes under the heading of 'cross disciplinary fertilization'. It means discussing a matter with someone in a totally different field. For instance a medical scientist might discuss systems behaviour with a business analyst or with a fashion designer. One can also listen to other people talking on their own subject.

    4. Physical exposure to random stimulation. This may involve wandering around an area which contains a multitude of different objects, for instance a general store like Woolworths or a toy shop. It may also mean going along to an exhibition which has nothing to do with the subject you are interested in.

The main point about the exposure method is to realize that one is *never looking for anything*. One could go to an exhibition to see if there was anything relevant. One could discuss a problem with someone in another field in order to hear their views on it. But that is *not* the purpose. If one goes looking for something relevant then one has preset ideas of relevance. And such preset ideas of relevance can only arise from the current way of looking at the situation. One wanders around with a completely blank mind and waits for something to catch one's attention. Even if nothing seems to catch one's attention there is still no effort to find something useful.

● Formal generation of random input

Because attention is a passive process even if one wanders around an exhibition without looking for anything relevant attention does tend to settle on items which have some relevance to the established way of looking at a situation. No matter how hard one tries to resist doing so one is still exerting some selection. This reduces the random nature of the input but still allows it to be very effective. In order to use truly random inputs one has to generate them deliberately. This seems paradoxical in so far as a random input is supposed to occur by chance. What one actually does is to set up a formal process to produce chance events. Shaking a pair of dice is such a situation. Three methods are suggested below :

1. Use of a dictionary to provide a random word.
2. Formal selection of a book or journal in a library.
3. The use of some routine to select an object from the surroundings (e.g. the nearest red object). The use of a dictionary will be described in more detail further on in this section. Formal selection of a book or journal simply means that one makes a point of picking up a journal from a particular position on the shelves no matter what the journal may be. One opens it and reads any one article in it no matter how remote these may seem. One can do the same thing with a book. These are but examples of how one can set up deliberate habits or routines in order to generate random inputs.

The effect of random stimulation

Why should random stimulation have any effect? Why should a totally unrelated piece of information help to bring about the restructuring of an established pattern?

Random stimulation only works because the mind functions as a self-maximizing memory system. In such a system there is a limited and *coherent* attention span.* This means that any two inputs cannot remain separate no matter how unconnected they are. Normally if there were two unconnected inputs one of them would be ignored and the other one would be attended to. But if both are deliberately held in attention (by deliberately arranging the setting) then a connection will eventually form between the two. At first there may be a rapid alternation of attention between the two items but soon the short term memory effect * will establish some sort of link.

In this type of system nothing can be truly irrelevant.

The established patterns on the memory surface are stable patterns. That does not mean that they do not change but that the pattern of change is stable. The flow of thought is stable. This equilibrium state is altered by the sudden inclusion of some new information.

Sometimes the new equilibrium state is very similar to the old one with a slight alteration to include the new information. At other times a complete restructuring comes about. There is a game in which plastic discs are placed within a frame one side of which is being forced inward by a spring. The pressure of this spring forces the plastic discs together to give a stable structure. Each player in turn removes a plastic disc. Usually the pattern shifts slightly to achieve a new equilibrium state. But sometimes there is a big change and the whole pattern is restructured. With a random input one is putting something in instead of taking it out but the shift in equilibrium occurs in the same way.

Random stimulation can work in two other ways. The random input can bring about a new entry point to the problem under consideration. The diagram below suggests a situation and the natural way this situation would develop. A random input is then added and a connection develops between the situation and the random input. As a result a new entry point is provided and the line of development of the original situation may be altered.

random stimulus

A random input can also work as an analogy. A single word from a dictionary provides a situation which has its own line of development. When this is related to the development of the problem being considered one has the analogy effect described in a previous chapter.

Random word stimulation

This is a practical and definite procedure in which the true random nature of the input is beyond doubt. If one is a purist one can use a table of random numbers to select a page in a dictionary. The number of a word on that page (counting down the page) can also be obtained from the table of random numbers. With less trouble one can simply think of two numbers and find the word that way. Or throw some dice. What one must not do is to open a dictionary and go through the pages until one finds a likely looking word. That would be selection and it would be useless from a random stimulation point of view.

The numbers 473-13 were given by a table of random numbers and using the Penguin English Dictionary the word located was: 'noose'. The problem under consideration was 'the housing shortage'. Over a timed three minute period the following ideas were generated:

noose - tightening noose - execution - what are the difficulties in executing a housing programme - what is the bottleneck, is it capital, labour or land?

noose tightens - things are going to get worse with the present rate of population increase.

noose - rope - suspension construction system - tentlike houses but made of permanent materials - easily packed and erected - or on a large scale with several houses suspended from one framework - much lighter materials possible if walls did not have to support themselves and the roof.

noose - loop - adjustable loop - what about adjustable round houses which could be expanded as required - just uncoil the walls - no point in having houses too large to begin with because of heating problems, extra attention to walls and ceilings, furniture etc. - but facility for slow stepwise expansion as need arises.

noose - snare - capture - capture a share of the labour market - capture - people captured by home ownership due to difficulty in selling and complications - lack of mobility - houses as exchangeable units - classified into types - direct exchange of one type for similar type - or put one type into the pool and take out a similar type elsewhere.

Some of the above ideas may be useful, others may not. All of them could have been arrived at by straightforward vertical thinking but that does not mean that they would have been arrived at this way. As discussed before if an idea is tenable at all then it must be possible in hindsight to see how it could have been arrived at by logical means but this does not mean that it would have been arrived at in this way. Sometimes the link to the random word may be effected after the idea has come to mind rather than the random word stimulating the idea. Nevertheless the use of the random word has stimulated a large number of different ideas in a short period of time.

From this example may be seen the way the random word is

used. Often the random word is used to generate further words which themselves link up with the problem being considered. Examples of this include: noose – execution – bottleneck; noose – rope – suspension; noose – snare – capture. A chain of ideas stretches out from the random word in order to effect a link with the problem. At times the functional properties of a noose were transferred to the problem: tightening noose, adjustable, round. The random word can be used in these and in many other ways. *There is no one correct way to use it.* In some cases a pun on the word may be used, or its opposite, or the word spelled slightly differently. The word is used in order to get things going – not to prove anything. Not even to prove that random word stimulation is useful.

● Time allowed

In the above example the time allowed was three minutes. This is quite long enough to stimulate ideas. If one sits around with a word long enough then it can become boring. With practice and confidence three minutes should be enough or at most five minutes. What one must not do is to immediately look for another random word at the end of the period because this tends to set up a search routine in which one goes through word after word until one finds a suitable one. Suitable would only mean one that fits in with the established views of the situation. If one wants to try another word it should be on another occasion. Knowing that one is going to move directly to another word (and hopefully a better one) reduces the effectiveness of the first word. Even after the end of the fixed period further ideas will occur. One can note them down. But there is no question of going through the rest of the day desperately trying to extract the maximum from the random word. One can get into the habit of using a random word on a problem for three minutes every day.

● Confidence

The most important factor in the successful use of random stimu-lation is confidence. There is no sense of urgency or effort but a quiet confidence that something will emerge. It is difficult to build such confidence because at first ideas will be slow to come. But as one learns to handle random stimulation in the knowledge that nothing can be irrelevant it becomes easier and easier.

Practice

1. Relating a random word

A problem is stated and written out on the blackboard. The students are then asked for suggestions of a number up to the number of pages in a dictionary (e.g. a number from 1 to 460) and then for another number to give the position of the word on that page (e.g. 1 to 20). Using a dictionary the corresponding word is located. The word is written down together with its meaning (unless the word is a very familiar one). The students are then asked for suggestions as to how the word could be related to the problem. To begin with the teacher may have to make most of the suggestions himself until the students get used to the process. Each suggestion is elaborated briefly but no attempt is made to note down the suggestions. The session goes on for 5 to 10 minutes.

Possible problems:

How to deal with the problem of shoplifting.

Increasing car safety.

A new design for windows to make them easier to open and close without the danger of people falling out or draughts.

New design for a lampshade.

Unless the teacher is fairly confident about his ability to use *any* random words it might be better to use the list given below rather than a dictionary. In this case the class would be asked for a number from 1 to 20.

1. weed
2. rust
3. poor
4. magnify
5. foam
6. gold
7. frame
8. hole

9. diagonal
10. vacuum
11. tribe
12. puppet
13. nose
14. link

15. drift
16. duty
17. portrait
18. cheese
19. chocolate
20. coal

2. Same problem, different words

Here a problem is set but different random words are used. Each student works on his own and makes notes of how the word generates ideas about the problem. At the end the results are collected. If there is time these are analysed to see whether there is any consistency of approach which depends on the random word used. The same idea may have been reached in different ways depending on the random word. If there is not much time then some of the results are selected at random and read out. One can also take the end idea in each chain of thought and then ask the class to imagine what the random word was in this particular case and the line of thought that led to it. (e.g.) if the problem was 'holidays' and the random word was 'turkey' a chain of thought might run: turkey – special food – Christmas – special holiday – more holidays with a special purpose. One would just take the 'more holidays with a special purpose' and ask what the random word might have been.

Two or three random words distributed among the class would be enough. More would just be confusing. The words can be taken from a dictionary or from the list above.

Possible problems might include:

Clearing oil off a beach.

Weeding the garden.

Design of apparatus for rescuing people from a burning building.

Making plastic sheet suitable for clothing (how would one treat it to make it hang properly).

3. Same word, different problems

This may be done either as an individual practice session or as an open class session. A random word is selected and then each student is given one out of two or three chosen problems. The student works to relate that random word to the problem he has been assigned. At the end the results are compared to show the different uses of the same word.

At an open class session three problems are listed. The random word is then related to each of the three problems in turn. Five minutes are spent on each problem. Suggestions are volunteered by the students and the teacher adds his own whenever there is a pause. It is better if the three problems are not written up together for then some students might be thinking ahead to the next problem.

Possible random words:
drain
engine
cooking
leaf

Possible problems:
How to store information so that it is easily available.
How to spend less time learning a subject.
A device to help you climb trees.
Design for a better cinema.

4. Your own problems

The students each write down any problem they would like to tackle. They write it down in duplicate, put a name or number on each sheet, and give one copy to the teacher. This is to prevent a sudden change in the problem when the random word is given. A random word is then found (by page number etc. suggested by the students to locate a word in the dictionary or just chosen by the teacher).

Before they hand in their results some of the students are asked by the teacher to describe to the rest of the class how they related the word to their own problem. In this type of session one can get an idea of how the same random word can be of use in many different situations. If some students find that they cannot make any progress at all then the teacher goes through the problem with them showing how the random word might be used in each case.

Possible random words:
scrambled eggs

screwdriver
bomb
doorhandle
  5. Random objects
  The objects are not random to the teacher who selects them
but to the students to whom they are presented. The advantage of
an object over a word is that an actual object can be looked at in
many more ways than the word describing that object. One
should be able to *imagine* an object in just as much detail but in
practice one does not and the function of the object tends to
swamp the other features. A problem is given to the students and
then the random object is presented. This can either be run as an
open class session with the students making suggestions as to how
the object may be related to the problem or it can be done on an
individual basis with comment on the results or individual
students describing their own results.
  Possible objects include:
a shoe
a tube of toothpaste
a newspaper
an apple
a sponge
a glass of water
  Possible problems might include:
Learning how to swim.
A new design for clocks.
A device for getting handicapped people in and out of bed.
Unblocking a drain.

Summary

If one only works from within an established pattern then one
tends to follow its natural line of development and is unlikely to
restructure the pattern. Usually one waits patiently for chance
circumstances to provide information that will trigger off an
insight restructuring. With random stimulation one deliberately

mixes in an unconnected piece of information in order to disturb the original pattern. From this disturbance may come a restructuring of the pattern or at least a new line of development. For the random input to be effective there must be no selection about it for as soon as there is selection there is relevance and the disturbing effect of the random input is reduced. Random stimulation is a provocation. Because of the way the mind works any stimulus whatsoever can be found to develop a connection with any other.

Division

A limited and coherent attention span arises directly from the mechanics of the self-maximizing memory surface that is mind. This limited attention span means that one only reacts to a bit of the total environment. Over a period of time one bit may be attended to after another until the total environment is covered.

In effect the total, continuous and overwhelming environment is divided up into separate attention areas. The process may involve picking out a single attention area or it may involve dividing up the environment into a number of attention areas. This is shown in the diagram below. There is no basic difference between

the two processes except that one covers the whole field and the other does not.

Although this process arises directly from the mechanics of the system it has several very useful advantages.

1. It means that some part of the environment can be reacted to specifically. Thus if the total environment contained something useful and something dangerous one could react differently to each part.

2. It means that new and unfamiliar environments can be dealt with by picking out features that are familiar. Eventually the situation is explained in terms of such familiar parts.

3. It means that the separate parts can be moved around and combined in different ways to produce effects that are not available in the environment.

4. It makes communication possible because a situation can be described bit by bit instead of as a whole.

Separation into units, selection of units, and combination of units in different ways together provide a very powerful information processing system. All these functions follow directly from the mechanism of mind.

● Reassembly

The previous diagram shows how units can be created by dividing up a total situation. Units can however also be created by putting together other units to form a new one that is then treated as a complete unit.

Words, names, labels

When a unit is obtained by dividing up a total situation or by putting together other units it is convenient to 'fix' that unit by giving it a separate name. The name is separate and unique to itself. The name establishes it as a pattern in its own right instead of just being part of another pattern. Having a name gives a unit much greater mobility since it now becomes more sharply divided off from its neighbours and comes to exist on its own. A name is especially useful for combining different units together to give a new one. The new unit only exists in so far as it is given a name. Without that name it would dissolve back into its separate parts.

The use of names for units is essential for communication. Names make it possible to transfer a complex situation a piece at a time.

To be of any use in communication the names must be fixed and permanent. Once a name is assigned to a unit then the shape of that unit is 'frozen' because the name itself does not change. This fixity of name is vital for communication and it is also useful for understanding a situation. In understanding however one does not actually have to use names though most people find it convenient to do so.

Myths
Myths are patterns which first arise in the mind. Once these patterns have formed something may be found in the environment which justifies them or else they dictate the way the environment is looked at and so achieve a pseudo-justification. Once one has names then one can do things to the names themselves and so produce more names. Thus if one has a word one can produce a word with an opposite meaning merely by adding 'un'. One can then look around to see what this new word fits or use it anyway whether it represents anything or not. Similarly once one has two words one can put them together to give a third word which is a combination of the other two. Both these processes are shown overleaf. These new units are created on the word level rather than derived from the environment. Yet these myth words are treated in exactly the same way as ordinary words which do refer to actual things in the environment. Instead of the myth word following something in the environment the myth word comes first and actually 'produces' something in the environment (by dictating the way one looks at something). Both sorts of words have the same degree of permanence and reality. Both are treated in exactly the same way.

Limitations of the naming system
The great practical advantage of the named unit system is its permanence and the great practical disadvantage of the named unit system is its permanence.

Names, labels, words, are themselves fixed and permanent.

Hence the units which have been taken over by these names have also to be fixed and permanent. Hence the patterns which are arrangements of such units tend also to be fixed and permanent.

The major disadvantage is that a named unit which might have been very convenient at one time may no longer be convenient,

indeed it may be restricting. The named assemblies of units (which are called concepts) are even more restricting because they impose a rigid way of looking at a situation. When there is a famine in a rice eating country and maize is sent in by other countries the starving people prefer to starve. Such is the rigidity of the concept, 'maize is food for animals'.

Even without a name a concept would be fixed by repeated use and growing familiarity. Putting a label on it accelerates the process.

Some of the limitations that arise from this named unit process are outlined below.

1. A division at a point of convenience produces two units which then become established and named. Subsequently it may be more convenient to divide the original situation into three units. This is shown in the top figure opposite. The establishment of the new units is very difficult as it means carving bits out of

the previous units and putting them together so that they form a new unit rather than revert back to the old units.

2. The lower figure shows how an assembly of units becomes established as a new unit. If it becomes more convenient to change this assembly so that it includes some new units but excludes some old ones this is very difficult.

3. When a unit is separated out and named it is difficult to realize that it is part of a whole.

4. When an assembly of units is given an overall name it may be difficult to realize that it is made up of parts.

5. When a division has been made it is difficult to bridge across that division. If a process has been cut at some point and what goes before that point is called 'cause' and what comes after is called 'effect' then it is difficult to bridge across the point and call the whole thing 'change'.

This is not a comprehensive list by any means. What is implied is that if units have been cut out and assembled in various ways which are then fixed by labels it becomes very difficult to use different units or different ways of putting them together.

Polarization

It is easier to establish two completely different patterns than to change an established pattern. If a new pattern is only slightly different then it will shift towards the established pattern. There is a tendency for established patterns to 'mop up' similar patterns which are treated as a repetition of the standard pattern. This results in a distortion of the information that is actually presented. The pattern that would have been established by the information is shifted towards an established pattern. If there are two established patterns then the shift may be towards one or other. If the two established patterns are opposite 'poles' in any sense then this shifting moves the new pattern towards one or other pole.

It is like having two wooden boxes side by side into which one is putting ping-pong balls. The balls have to go into one box or the other. A ball will not balance on the division between the two boxes. If the edges of the boxes are sloping then the ball may be moved quite a long way. The process is suggested by the diagram below.

black   white

If one of the boxes is labelled 'black balls' and the other one 'white balls' then each ball is dropped into the appropriate box depending on whether it is black or white. If there are any grey balls then some sort of decision has to be made as to whether they go into the black box or the white box. Once the decision is made the balls go into the white box just as if they were white or into the black box just as if they were black. The apparent nature of the ball has been shifted to make it fit in with the established pattern.

A whole series of boxes might be imagined, each with its own label. As each item came along it would be put into whichever box had the most appropriate label. It would not matter if this most appropriate label was not really very appropriate. There is a shift to fit in with whatever labels are available. Once the shift has been made then it is impossible to tell that the item in the box is any different from the other items in the box.

In order to find an appropriate box for any item that does not fit readily into any available box one can do two things. One can concentrate on those points which show that it ought to fit into one box. Or one can concentrate on those points which show that it should *not* fit into a particular box. Thus with the grey ping-pong balls one might have said, 'Grey is almost white therefore it fits into the white box' or one might have said, 'Black is a true absence of any colour therefore the grey ball cannot go into the black box.'

If two things are similar one could notice the points of similarity and say the two things are the same or one could notice the points of difference and say the two things are different. The two things would be shifted together to be similar or shifted apart to be different. Either way there would be some shift as suggested in the diagram.

Similarly when there is an established label a new item is either pushed right under that label or else pushed right out. In a community that is sharply divided into 'us' and 'them' any stranger who happens along is assessed as to whether he is 'one of us' or 'one of them'.

Probably the stranger has a mixture of characteristics which would make him fit either group. But whichever way the decision goes his characteristics are at once assumed to have changed so that they match exactly the characteristics of the label. The stranger is pushed towards one or other pole. He cannot remain in between any more than the needle of a compass can remain undecided when a magnet is brought near to it.

From a practical point of view this polarizing system is very effective. What it means is that one can establish a few major categories and then push everything into one or other of these. Instead of having to assess everything in detail and then decide how one is going to react one merely assesses whether it fits into one category or another. This is not even a matter of exact fit but of pushing it one way or another. Once the thing has been pushed into a category then reaction is easy since the categories are established and so is the reaction to them.

In exploring a new situation one might have two categories: 'good to eat' and 'bad to eat'. This is sufficient. Anything examined can be pushed one way or the other. There is no need to have any subtle distinctions. Such distinctions as: 'tastes nasty but is good for one', or 'good to eat but makes one very thirsty', or 'tastes good but is poisonous', 'not known but worth trying' are excluded.

● New categories

At what point does a new category arise? At what point does one decide that the item will not fit into any of the boxes and so create a new box? At what point does one decide that grey ping-pong balls would go into a special box marked 'grey'? At what point is it decided that the stranger is neither 'we' nor 'they' but something else?

The danger of polarization is that things can be shifted around so much that there never comes a point when a new category *has to be created*. Nor is there any indication as to how many established categories there should be.

One can get by with very few categories.

The dangers of the polarizing tendency may now be summarized:

● Once established the categories become permanent.

● New information is altered so that it fits an established category. Once it has done so there is no indication that it is any different from anything else under that category.

● At no point is it ever *essential* to create new categories. One can get by with very few categories.

● The fewer the categories the greater the degree of shift.

Lateral thinking

There is no question that the named unit system is highly effective. There is no question that the polarizing properties of this system make it possible to react with very little information. The whole information processing system that arises from the basic mechanism of mind is immensely useful. The disadvantages mentioned above are minor ones compared to the usefulness of the system. But the disadvantages do exist. Moreover they are inseparable from the nature of the system. So one uses the system to its full effectiveness but at the same time realizes the errors and tries to do something about them.

The major limitation of the named unit system is the rigidity of the labels. Once established the labels are fixed. The labels alter the incoming information instead of the incoming information altering the labels.

The aim of lateral thinking is to break out of cliché patterns and rigid labels are a perfect example of cliché patterns. In order to escape from these labels one can do three things:

● Challenge the labels.

● Try and do without them.

● Establish new labels.

● Challenging the labels

Why am I using this label?
What does it really mean?
Is it essential?
Am I just using it as a convenient cliché?
Why do I have to accept that label used by other people?

As it implies, challenging a label means a direct challenge to the use of a label, a word, or a name. It does not mean that one disagrees with its use or that one has any better alternative. It just means that one is not prepared to accept the cliché label without challenging it.

It is not a matter of seeking justification for the label so that one can continue to use it. One continues to challenge the label all the time even when one is using it.

● Trying to do without labels

Whenever units are assembled together and given a new name or label this becomes so easily established that one tends to forget what lies underneath the label. By abolishing the label one can rediscover what there is underneath. One may find much of use that was hitherto hidden. One may find that there is very little of importance even though the label itself seemed to be important. One may find that the label is indeed useful but that it needs to be changed to bring it up to date.

By abolishing the label one abolishes the cliché convenience of the label. If one is writing or speaking one tries to proceed without the cliché convenience of that label — without that label. Whenever one comes to a point when one would normally use the label one has to find a way of doing without it. This may involve finding another way of looking at things and this of course is the aim of lateral thinking. It is not much use substituting some phrase instead of the label but it is still of some use because the phrase can interact with other things in the way a fixed label cannot.

A simple example of trying to do without a label would be rewriting a very personal piece in which 'I' occurred all the time. In rewriting it to avoid the use of 'I' one would find that many things would have happened anyway and that the personal involvement was much less than had seemed.

It is not only in discussing a situation that one tries to do without a particular label but also in looking at a situation. Using the label 'mob' it is easy to develop a certain line of thought but if one has to do without this label then one might be able to look at the situation in a different way. One tries to see things as they actually are and not in terms of labels.

● Establishing new labels

It may seem paradoxical to establish a new label in order to escape the harmful effects of labels. The purpose of establishing a new label is however to escape the distorting effects of the old labels. The polarizing effect tends to shift information into established categories. The fewer the categories the greater the shift and distortion. By establishing a new category one can accept information with less distortion. So one establishes a new label in order to protect incoming information from the polarizing effect of already established labels.

Established labels tend to build around themselves meanings, contexts and lines of development. Even if one wants to use an idea that would fit under an existing label it might be better not to put it there if one wants to develop the idea in a new way. For instance lateral thinking does overlap with what some people understand by creative thinking. But because creative thinking is surrounded by a whole complex of meanings including artistic expression, talent, sensitivity, inspiration etc. it is far better to establish lateral thinking as a separate idea if one wishes to regard it as a deliberate way of using information. Similarly the word 'patriotism' is so surrounded by heroics and duty and virtue and 'my country right or wrong' that one has to regard it as either very honourable or very dangerous. If one wants to encourage national spirit in terms of one country among others and in terms of individual culture and in terms of economic growth, then one needs a new label.

Practice

1. Challenging labels
This is rather similar to the 'why' technique described in a previous section. When one challenges a name, a label, or a concept one is *not asking for the term to be defined*. One is questioning the use of the term as a term, not asking for its justification or explanation.

An article is taken from a newspaper or magazine and read out to the students. If there are enough copies they can be asked to read it for themselves. The task is to pick out certain labels which seem to be used too glibly. Each of these labels is underlined. It may be a label or a concept that is fundamental to the whole argument or it may be a label that is used very often. For instance in an article on management the labels picked out might include 'productivity', 'profitability', 'coordination'. Each student makes a list of such cliché words and at the end the lists are compared and discussed. The discussion is focused on how these labels are being used in too convenient a fashion. The point is not that the labels are right or wrong but that it is too convenient to write 'profitability' whenever one has to justify something. In another article the cliché words might be 'justice', 'equality', 'human rights'. In addition to discussing why the label is being used too glibly one also discusses the danger of using labels in this way.

2. Labels and discussion

Two students are asked to debate a subject while the rest of the students listen. At the end the other students comment on the use of labels during the discussion. It is enough that the students become aware of the easy use of labels. It is not a matter of deciding whether the label was justified nor a matter of commenting on debating techniques.

Possible subjects for such a discussion might include:

Are women as creative as men?

How far is obedience a good thing?

One should only learn subjects which are going to be immediately useful.

If you don't get what you want you should go on trying.

Parents should help children with their homework.

Children should dress as they like at school.

Some people are different from others.

3. Dropping labels

Here it is a matter of seeing how well one can do without a particular name or label or concept. The label is dropped completely and the article is rewritten without the use of that label.

It is convenient to do this with newspaper articles that make much use of some particular label. In commenting on the result the teacher notes whether dropping the label has caused the thing to be looked at in a different way or whether the label has been replaced by a cliché phrase instead.

4. Dropping labels in discussion

Here one student is asked to discuss a subject. Then another student is asked to explain what the first student has said but without using some particular label used by the first student. This type of thing can also be done with a debate between students with both sides forbidden to use some label. It can also be done with only one of the sides forbidden to use the label.

Possible subjects for discussion:

War (with label of fighting dropped).
Car racing (with label of fast, speedy, etc dropped).
Walking in the rain (with label of wet dropped).
School (with label of teaching dropped).
Police (with label of law dropped).

5. Rephrasing

Instead of dropping a concept label in the course of a discussion or rewriting an article one practises doing it with single sentences. This is rather more simple to do than the previous exercise and it can be very useful practice. The teacher selects a series of sentences which may be taken from newspapers or just made up. The sentences are read out or written up on the board. The label which is to be dropped is underlined. The students can then offer suggestions in open class as to how the sentence could be rephrased without that word. Alternatively they can each produce a version of the sentence and at the end the different versions can be compared. The important point with this exercise is that the meaning must be kept as intact as possible.

The type of sentence which could be used is as follows:

Children should be as *tidy* as possible in their homework.
Everyone has the right to *equal opportunity* in education.
In a democracy government is by the *will* of the people.
If a thief is caught *stealing* he may be sent to prison.

Strawberry ice cream *tastes* better than vanilla.

If you drop a *plate* on the floor it will break.

The difficulty with this type of exercise is that very often one simply gets synonyms. Thus in the above examples one might well get 'careful', or 'neat' instead of the word 'tidy'. One cannot really refuse to accept synonyms for the dividing line is very difficult between what is a genuine synonym and what is a different way of looking at the situation. So one accepts synonyms but goes on further and asks for further ways of putting things. Instead of refusing them one tries to exhaust synonyms.

6. Headlines

This is very similar to the previous exercise. Instead of sentences a series of headlines is taken from the newspapers. The task is to rephrase the entire headline so that no one word is the same as before and yet the meaning is the same. It is necessary to choose headlines which do not have specific labels in them. For instance the headline 'Ribofillo wins Derby' would be difficult to rephrase unless one were allowed to say, 'Favourite triumphs in classic Epsom race', but this would imply that one knew Ribofillo to be the favourite. One has to allow some licence in this respect.

7. New labels

Since communication is so very important one does not really want to encourage students to develop their own special labels for things. One can however have an open class session in which the students are asked to put forward ideas which they feel are:

1. Improperly classified.

2. Left out by existing labels.

For instance someone may feel that a hovercraft is not really an aeroplane or a car but something special. Someone else might feel that 'guilty' and 'innocent' are too sharp a division and that there should be room for a person who is technically guilty but innocent as far as intention goes (or technically innocent but actually guilty).

Perhaps there ought to be a special label for something which is not 'ugly' or 'beautiful' instead of having to call it ordinary. Perhaps there ought to be a special label to cover the phrase, 'the way you look at something'. Perhaps there ought to be a special label for something that was going well at the moment, but was clearly headed for disaster. Perhaps there ought to be a special label for something that was not entirely an accident nor was it entirely someone's fault but a mixture of the two.

Understanding the nature of lateral thinking and the need for it is the first step towards using it. But understanding and goodwill are not enough. The formal routines suggested as methods of applying lateral thinking are more practical but there is a great need for something more definite, more simple, and more universal. Some tool for applying lateral thinking just as NO is a tool for applying logical thinking.

NO and PO

The concept of logical thinking is selection and this is brought about by the processes of acceptance and rejection. Rejection is the basis of logical thinking. The rejection process is incorporated in the concept of the negative. The negative is a judgement device. It is the means whereby one rejects certain arrangements of information. The negative is used to carry out judgement and to indicate rejection. The concept of the negative is crystallized into a definite language tool. This language tool consists of the words no and not. Once one learns the function and use of these words one has learned how to use logical thinking. The whole concept of logical thinking is concentrated in the use of this language tool. Logic could be said to be the management of NO.

The concept of lateral thinking is insight restructuring and this is brought about through the rearrangement of information. Rearrangement is the basis of lateral thinking and rearrangement means escape from the rigid patterns established by experience.

The rearrangement process is incorporated in the concept of the (re) laxative. The laxative is a rearranging device. It is the means whereby one can escape from established patterns and create new ones. The laxative allows the arrangement of information in new ways from which new patterns can arise. The concept of the laxative is crystallized into a definite language tool. This language tool is PO. Once one learns the function and use of PO one has learned how to use lateral thinking. The whole concept of lateral thinking is concentrated in the use of this language tool. Lateral thinking could be said to be the management of PO just as logical thinking is the management of NO.

PO is to lateral thinking what NO is to logical thinking. NO is a rejection tool. PO is an insight restructuring tool. The concept of the laxative is the basis of lateral thinking just as the concept of the negative is the basis of logical thinking. Both concepts have to be crystallized into language devices. It is essential to have language devices because of the passive nature of the mechanism of mind. The language devices are themselves patterns which interact with other patterns on the self-organizing memory surface of mind to bring about certain effects. Such language devices are extremely useful in one's own thinking and for communication they are essential.

Although both NO and PO function as language tools the operations they carry out are totally different. NO is a judgement device. PO is an anti-judgement device. NO works within the framework of reason. PO works outside that framework. PO may be used to produce arrangements of information that are unreasonable but they are not really unreasonable because lateral thinking functions in a different way from vertical thinking. Lateral thinking is not irrational but arational. Lateral thinking deals with the patterning of information not with the judgement of those patterns. Lateral thinking is prereason. PO is never a judgement device. PO is a construction device. PO is a patterning device. The patterning process may also involve depatterning and repatterning.

Although PO is a language tool it is at the same time an anti-language device. Words themselves are just as much cliché patterns as the way they are put together. PO provides a temporary escape from the discrete and ordered stability of language which reflects the established patterns of a self-organizing memory system. That is why the full function of PO is unlikely to have evolved in the development of language. Instead PO arises from consideration of the patterning behaviour of the mind.

The function of PO is the arrangement of information to create new patterns and to restructure old ones.

These two functions are but different aspects of the same process but for convenience they may be separated.

● Creating new patterns.
● Challenging old patterns.

These two functions can be expressed in another way:

● Provocative and permissive: putting information together in new ways and allowing unjustified arrangements of information.
● Liberating: disrupting old patterns in order to allow the imprisoned information to come together in a new way.

The first function of PO: creating new arrangements of information

Experience arranges things in patterns. Things in the environment may happen to be arranged in a particular pattern or else attention may pick things out in a certain pattern. In one case the pattern is derived from the environment and in the other case it is derived from the memory surface of mind since this directs attention. The first function of PO is to create arrangements of information that do not arise from either of these two sources. Just as NO is used to weaken arrangements that are based on experience so PO is used to generate connections that have nothing to do with experience.

Once information has 'settled' into fixed patterns on the memory surface* then new arrangements can only occur if they are directly derived from these patterns. Only such trial arrangements of information are allowed as would be consistent with these background patterns. Anything else is dismissed at once. Yet if (somehow) different arrangements of information could be brought about and held for a short while then the information might snap together to form a new pattern that was either consistent with the background pattern or capable of altering it. This process is shown diagrammatically overleaf. The purpose of PO is then either to bring about arrangements that would otherwise not occur or to protect from dismissal arrangements that would otherwise be dismissed as impossible. These functions may be listed as follows:

To arrange information in a way which would never have come about in the normal course of events.

To hold an arrangement of information without judging it.

To protect from dismissal an arrangement of information which has already been judged as impossible.

An arrangement of information is usually judged as soon as it comes about. The judgement results in one of two verdicts: 'This is permissible', or 'This is not permissible'. The arrangement is either affirmed or denied. There is no middle course. The function of PO is to introduce a middle course as suggested in the diagram. PO is never a judgement. It does not quarrel with the verdict but with the very application of the judgement. PO is an anti-judgement device.

PO allows one to hold an arrangement for a little longer without having to affirm or deny it. PO delays judgement.

The usefulness of delaying judgement is one of the most basic principles of lateral thinking. It is also one of the fundamental points of difference from vertical thinking. With vertical thinking an arrangement of information must be right at every _tep, which means that one must use judgement at the earliest possible opportunity. With lateral thinking an arrangement of information may be wrong in itself but can lead to a perfectly valid new idea. This possibility arises directly from consideration of the mind as a self-maximizing memory surface.

By delaying judgement and holding onto an idea a number of things may happen. If the idea is pursued far enough it may be found to make sense. If one holds onto the idea then freshly arrived information can interact with the idea to give a valid idea. The unjudged idea may direct the search for information that can prove useful in its own right. Finally if the idea is held long enough then the context into which it did not fit may itself be changed.

Exactly the same considerations apply to the use of PO for protection of arrangements of information that have already been judged and dismissed. Such dismissed arrangements may have been dismissed long ago and it may be a matter of resurrecting them under the protection of PO. On the other hand the arrangements may have been proposed and dismissed only recently.

It is important to realize that the use of PO for creating new arrangements of information is quite different from the use of the usual devices for arranging information.

PO does not have an addition function as provided by 'and'.

PO does not have an identity function as provided by 'is'.

PO does not have an alternative function as provided by 'or'.

The function of PO *is to bring about a provocative arrangement of information without saying anything at all about it.* The arrangement itself is not important but what happens next is. The purpose of the arrangement is to lead forward to new ideas.

In practice there are certain specific occasions on which it is convenient to use PO.

● Juxtaposition

The simplest use of PO is to hold two unrelated things together in order to allow them or their associations to interact. No connection or relationship at all is implied between the two things. Nor is there any reason for putting them together (except what might happen). Without the PO device one would not easily be able to put things together in this way without finding, suggesting, or forcing some reason.

One might say, 'computers PO omelettes'. From this juxtaposition might come such ideas as: Cooking by computer or by some pre-set automatic device. Another idea would be a central store of recipes and one would use a telephone to dial in your ingredients and requirements in order to be given a matched recipe. Both omelettes and computers are concerned with the changing of raw material into a more usable form. In an omelette things are mixed up but come out in a definite form so with a certain type of computer an apparently random mixing of information would still result in some definite output (as for instance in the brain).

● Introduction of a random word

Instead of linking two unconnected words together as in juxtaposition PO can be used to 'introduce' a random unconnected word into a discussion in order to stimulate new ideas. You could say, 'Gentlemen, you know all about lateral thinking and the use of a random input to help disturb cliché patterns of thought and to stimulate new ideas. I am now going to introduce such a random word. This word has no connection at all with what we have been discussing. There is no reason behind my choice of the word. The only reason for its use is the hope that it will provoke some new ideas. Do not feel that there really is a hidden reason. Do not spend your time searching for this reason. The word is 'raisin'. Instead of saying all that one would simply say: 'Po raisin'.

If the problem under discussion was, 'How to use study time' then this random word could set off such ideas as: raisin – used to make cakes enjoyable – small pockets of sweetness – intersperse short periods of more interesting subjects among longer periods of less interesting subjects – create small nodes of interest in less interesting subjects:

raisins – dried grapes – concentrated sweetness – concentrate and summarize material so that it can be taken in over a shorter time.

raisins – exposed in the sun to dry – perhaps one can study in a pleasant surrounding as easily as in an unpleasant one – do lighting, colour etc. affect boredom? Perhaps material can be subjected to 'glare' of analysis by someone else in order to reduce it to its essentials.

raisins – dried for preservation – notes and summaries easier to remember but need reconstituting with fluid (i.e. examples).

● Disconnected jumps

In vertical thinking one moves in sequential steps but in lateral thinking one can make disconnected jumps and then try and fill in the gaps. If you do this in the middle of a vertical thinking discussion then everyone else will be very confused as they try to find the logic behind this jump. In order to indicate that the jump is a lateral disconnected one you could preface your comment with PO. For instance in the discussion about study time you might say, 'Po time spent studying is time spent not doing other things.'

The jump may be only a small one within the same field or it may be a large one to an unconnected field. PO saves one the trouble of having to link the new remark to what has gone before. As usual PO implies, 'Don't look for the reason behind this. Let us just go forward and see what the *effect* of it is.'

● Doubt (semi-certainty)

Whenever a discussion gets blocked by the impossibility of proving a certain point PO can be used to open things up again. PO does not prove the point or deny it but it allows the point to be used in any way which will enable the discussion to keep going. One can then see what happens. It may be that nothing very useful comes of it and one realizes that the original point was not so vital after all. It may be that one can reach a solution and from this one can find another way back to the starting point without having to go through the doubtful point. It may be that one can only reach a solution through the doubtful point and so one comes to realize how vital this point is and therefore increases the effort to prove it. This particular use of PO is not very different from the ordinary use of 'if' or 'suppose'.

● Being wrong

In lateral thinking one does not mind being wrong on the way to a solution because it may be necessary to go through a wrong area in order to get to a position from which the correct path is visible. PO is an escort that allows one to move through the wrong area. PO does not make things right but it switches attention from why something is wrong to how it may be useful. In effect PO implies, 'I know this is wrong but I am going to put things this way in order to see where it leads me.'

In considering the problem of keeping the windscreen of a car free from dirt and water someone suggested that cars ought to be driven backwards since the back window was always much easier to see out of than the front window. In itself this is obviously nonsense since if one was going backwards that window would get just as dirty as the ordinary windscreen. Nevertheless the suggestion, 'Why not drive backwards' can lead on to such other ideas as indirect vision systems or some way of protecting the windscreen from head on exposure to mud and water.

In this example PO would be used in the following way. Someone would suggest driving backwards and this would be met with the response, 'That's nonsense, because . . .' The reply to this would be, 'Po why not drive backwards'? The purpose of PO would be to delay judgement – to hold the idea in mind for a few moments in order to see what could arise from it instead of dismissing it at once.

● Holding function

In addition to protecting an idea which is obviously wrong PO can be used to protect an idea from judgement. In this case the idea has not already been judged but is about to be subjected to critical analysis. PO is used to *delay* this. This function of PO is rather similar to its use for the introduction of a random stimulus. An ordinary remark or idea in the course of a discussion is turned by the use of PO into a catalyst. Used in such circumstances PO indicates : 'Let's not bother to analyse whether this is right or wrong – let us just see what ideas it will lead to.'

PO could be used by the person offering the idea or it could be used by anyone else. Thus if an evaluation of the idea was started someone could simply interject, 'Po . . .' This would mean, 'Let's hold off evaluation for the moment.'

● Construction

In school geometry a problem is often made easier to solve by adding some additional lines to the original figure. This process is similar to that involved in the story of the lawyer whose task it was to divide up eleven horses among three sons so that one of them got half of the horses, another got a quarter, and the third son got one sixth. What he did was to lend his own horse to the sons and then divided the twelve horses up, giving the first son six, the second three and the third two. He then took his own horse back again.

Here PO is used to add something to the problem or to change it in some other way. Changing the problem in this way can lead to new lines of development, new ways of looking at it. The purpose of changing the problem is *not* to rephrase it or put it in a better way but to alter it and see what happens next. For instance in considering the efficiency of the police in dealing with crime one might say, 'Po why not employ one-armed policemen?' Changing the problem in this way by adding the factor of 'one-armed policemen' would focus attention on the possible advantages of being one-armed and especially on the need to use brain and organization rather than muscle power.

Summary

There are many other ways in which PO can be used but the occasions listed above are enough to illustrate the *first* function of PO. This first function is quite simply to allow one to say anything one likes. PO allows one to arrange information in any way whatsoever. There need be no justification at all for such arrangement except PO.
Po two and two make five.
Po water flows uphill if it is coloured green.
Po lateral thinking is a waste of time.
Po men have souls and women have not.
Po it takes a lifetime to unlearn what has been learned in education.
  The first function of PO is to shift attention from the meaning of a statement and the reason for making it to the effect of the statement. With PO one looks forwards instead of backwards. Because any arrangement of information can lead on to other arrangements a statement can be very useful as a stimulus no matter how nonsensical it is in itself. And by being nonsensical one can arrange information in a way that is different from the established patterns – and so increase the chance of a permanent restructuring. With vertical thinking one is not allowed to do any of this. With vertical thinking one looks backwards at the reason for a statement, at the justification, at the meaning.
  The statement, 'Po water flows uphill if it is coloured green' is ridiculous but it could lead on to such ideas as: Why should the green colour make a difference? Why should adding colour make a difference? Is there anything one could add to water to make it

flow uphill? In fact there is. If one adds a very small amount of a special plastic then the water acts as a solid/liquid to such an extent that if you start pouring water out of a jug and then hold the jug upright the water will continue to siphon out, climbing up the side of the jug, flowing over the rim and down the outer side.

PO as a device allows one to use information in this way which is completely different from the ordinary use of information. One could use information in this way without PO but one would still be using the lateral concept which is incorporated in PO. The convenience of PO as an actual language device is that it clearly indicates that information is being used in this special way. Without such an indication there would be confusion as the listener would not know what was going on. A PO type statement inserted into an ordinary vertical thinking discussion without the use of PO would lead the listeners to suppose that the speaker was mad, lying, mistaken, stupid, ignorant or facetious. Apart from the inconvenience of being the recipient of such judgements there is the danger of being taken seriously. For instance, 'Po the house is on fire' is rather different from 'The house is on fire'. Furthermore if one does not use PO then the information is not used as a stimulus in the lateral manner.

The second function of PO: challenging old arrangements of information

The basic function of mind is to create patterns. The memory surface of mind organizes information into patterns. Or rather it allows information to organize itself into patterns.* The effect is just the same as if the mind picked things out of the environment and put them together to give patterns. Once formed these patterns become ever more firmly established because they direct attention. The effectiveness of mind depends entirely on the creation, the recognition and the use of patterns. The patterns have to be permanent to be of any use. Yet the patterns are not necessarily the only way of putting together the information contained in them – or even the best. The patterns are determined by the time of arrival of the information or by preceding patterns that have been accepted entire.

The second function of PO is to challenge these established patterns. PO is used as a freeing device to free one from the fixity of established ideas, labels, divisions, categories and classifications. The way PO is used can be summarized under the following headings:

● To challenge the arrogance of established patterns.

● To question the validity of established patterns.

● To disrupt established patterns and liberate information that can come together to give new patterns.

● To rescue information trapped by the pigeonholes of labels and classifications.

● To encourage the search for alternative arrangements of the information.

● Never a judgement

As suggested before, PO is never used as a judgement device. PO is never used to indicate whether an arrangement of information is right or wrong. PO is never used to indicate whether an arrangement of information is likely or unlikely or whether it is the best available at the moment. PO is a device to bring about an arrangement or rearrangement of information not a device to judge the new arrangements or condemn the old ones.

PO implies, 'That may be the best way of looking at things or putting the information together. That may even turn out to be the only way. But let us look around for other ways.'

With vertical thinking one is not allowed to challenge an idea unless one can show why it is wrong or else provide an alternative. If one provides an alternative one must somehow show why this alternative is preferable to the original idea as well as proving that the alternative is sound. With PO one has to do none of these things. One challenges the established order without necessarily being able to offer anything in its place or even to show any deficiency.

Judgement usually asks for justification of an idea. Justification of why an arrangement of information should be accepted. One wants to know why something has been put together in a certain way. With PO the emphasis is shifted away from this 'why' to 'where to'. One accepts the need to rearrange information in new ways. One takes a new arrangement and instead of trying to see where it has come from and whether it is justified one sees where it leads to – *what effect it can have*.

● The response to PO

The challenge of PO is not met by a fierce defence of why the established idea is indeed the best possible way of putting things together because PO does not attack an idea. PO is a challenge to try and think of other ways. The challenge of PO is met by generating different ways of looking at the situation. The more ways one can generate the more clearly it may be shown that the original idea was indeed the best one but that is no reason for refusing to try and generate other ways. If in generating these alternative ways a new and better way of looking at things turns up then that can only be a good thing. Even if the old idea is only altered slightly that is still a good thing. Even the possibility that there might be another way of looking at things is useful in itself in so far as it lessens the rigidity of the old idea and makes it more easily changed when change is due.

● Challenging cliché patterns

Any pattern that is at all useful is a cliché. The more useful it is the more of a cliché it tends to become. And the more of a cliché it is the more useful it may become. PO can be used to challenge any cliché. PO not only challenges the way concepts are arranged into patterns but the very concepts themselves. One always tends to think of clichés as arrangements of concepts but that the concepts themselves must be accepted as the building blocks of thought and so must themselves remain unaltered.

'Po freedom' challenges the very concept of freedom not the value or purpose of freedom.

'Po punishment' challenges the very concept of punishment not the circumstances under which it is used or the purpose for which it is used.

As suggested above it is the useful concepts that need challenging most. The less useful concepts are likely to be under perpetual challenge and reformation. But the usefulness of a useful concept protects it.

● Focusing

Since the cliché may refer to a particular concept or a phrase or to the whole idea it is helpful if one is specific about what is being challenged by PO. In order to do this one would repeat what is being challenged but preface it with PO.

'It is the function of education to train the mind and to pass on to it the knowledge of ages.'

To this one might reply : 'Po, train the mind' or 'Po the knowledge of ages,' or even just 'Po train'.

Used in this way PO can act as a *focusing* device to direct attention to some concept that is always taken for granted because there are other concepts which seem more open to reexamination.

● Alternatives

There are times when it is reasonable to try and find other ways of looking at a situation. This happens when the current approach is not satisfactory. PO is used as a demand to generate alternatives even when it is quite *unreasonable*. One goes on generating alternatives right up to the point of absurdity – and beyond. Since there is no good reason for generating alternatives under these circumstances one needs the artificial stimulus of PO which is a device that works outside of reason.

'It is spring and the bird is on the wing.'

'No. The wing is on the bird.'

'Po.'

'The bird and the wing both happen to be going along in the same direction.'

Used in this way PO is an invitation (or a demand) to generate alternative arrangements of the information. It is also used to justify those alternative arrangements by making it clear that they are offered as alternative arrangements and not necessarily better arrangements or even justified ones.

● Anti-arrogance

One of the most valuable functions of PO is as an anti-arrogance device. PO is a reminder of the behaviour of the memory surface of mind. PO is a reminder that a particular arrangement of information which seems inevitable may yet have come about in an arbitrary fashion. PO is a reminder that the illusion of certainty may be useful but that it cannot be absolute. PO is a reminder that certainty about a particular arrangement of information can never exclude the possibility of there being another arrangement. PO challenges dogmatism and absolutism. PO challenges the arrogance of any absolute statement or judgement or point of view.

Used in this way PO does not imply that the statement is wrong. It does not even imply that the person using PO has doubts about the statement let alone justified doubts. All PO implies is that the statement is being made with a degree of arrogance that is not justified under any circumstances.

PO implies the following: 'You may be right and your logic may be faultless. Nevertheless you are starting from perceptions that are arbitrary and you are using concepts that are arbitrary since both are derived from your own individual experience or the general experience of a particular "culture". There are also the limitations of the information processing system of mind. You may be right within a particular context or using particular concepts but these are not absolute.'

PO used in this fashion is never intended to introduce so much doubt that an idea becomes unusable. PO is never directed at an idea itself but only at the arrogance surrounding it – at the exclusion of other possibilities.

● Counteracting NO

NO is a very convenient device for handling information. It is a very definite and a very absolute device. NO also tends to be a permanent label. The permanence of the label, its definiteness and its absolute rejection, may rest on evidence that was at best flimsy. Once the label is applied however then the full force of the label takes over and the bare adequacy of the reason behind its application is lost. It may also happen that the label was justified when it was originally applied but that things have changed and the label is now no longer justified. Unfortunately the label remains until it is removed – it does not only last so long as there are reasons for it to last. Nor is it easy to examine whether there are sufficient reasons for maintaining the label because one cannot know whether a label is worth reexamining until one has in fact done so and the NO label itself deters such examination.

PO is used to counteract the absolute block caused by the NO label. As usual PO is not a judgement. PO does not imply that the NO label is incorrect nor does it even suggest that there is doubt about the label. In effect PO implies: 'Let us cover up that NO label for the moment and proceed as if it was not there.' As one goes forward with one's examination it may become obvious that the label is no longer justified. On the other hand it may become obvious that the label is still as valid as ever but nevertheless information which has been hidden behind the label may be very useful elsewhere.

Consider the statement: 'You cannot live if your heart stops.' This would be changed to 'Po you can live if your heart stops' and this leads on to consideration of the artificial devices for keeping a heart beating, for artificial hearts or transplanted hearts. It also leads on to the need for a new criterion of death since the heart can be kept beating by artificial means even when the brain is irreversibly damaged.

The history of science is full of instances when something was said not to be possible but later proved to be possible. Heavier than air flying machines are an example. In 1941 someone showed that to get a load weighing one pound to the moon would require a rocket weighing one million tons. Eventually the rocket that actually sent men to the moon weighed far less.

Any definite use of the NO label is an invitation to use PO.

● Anti-division

In so far as PO is used to challenge concepts it also challenges the division which divides something into two separate concepts. PO challenges not only the concepts but the division that has brought them about. The pattern making tendency of mind can both put together things that ought to be separated and also separate things that ought to be put together. Both an artificial difference and an artificial sameness may be challenged with PO.

If two things are separated by a division then PO may challenge the division or may shift attention towards the features which the two things have in common and away from those features that separate them.

Rigid divisions, classifications, categories and polarizations all have a great usefulness but they can also be limiting. As with NO the function of PO is to temporarily lift the labels and let the information come together again for reassessment. Information is dragged out of pigeonholes and allowed to interact. Things may be classified by a particular feature or by a particular function. Once classified the label becomes permanent and as a result all the other features and functions tend to be forgotten. One does not think of looking under a label for a function that is not indicated on that label. As in a filing system something is more effectively lost if it is misfiled than if it is not filed at all.

A spade and a broom are two very different things. 'Spade po broom' focuses attention on the similarities: in both a function is performed at the end of a shaft, both have long shafts, both can be used in a right-handed or a left-handed manner, in both there is a wide part at the end of the narrow part, both can be used for removing material from a place, both could be used as a weapon, both could be used to prop a door open etc.

'Artist po technologist.' One is very ready to put people into pigeonholes and the further the pigeonholes are apart the more useful they seem to be. They seem to be more useful because with far apart pigeonholes one finds it easier to predict what a person is going to do than if the pigeonholes overlapped. 'Artist po technologist' challenges the big gap there is supposed to be between the two types. It suggests that the two types may both be trying to do the same thing: to achieve an effect. The materials may be different but the methods may be the same: a combination of experience, information, experimentation and judgement. It may also suggest that nowadays an artist has to be something of a technologist if he is to use the newer media.

● Diversion

PO challenges concepts, it challenges the division between concepts, and it can also be used to challenge the line of development of a concept. Sometimes the line of development of an idea is so natural and so obvious that one moves quite smoothly along this path before ever wondering whether there might be an alternative path to be explored. To prevent this PO may be used as a temporary blocking device. PO is used as a special sort of NO but without the judgement of NO or the permanence of NO. In effect PO implies: 'That is the natural path of development but we are going to block that path for the moment in order to make it possible to explore some other pathways.'

'A business exists to make profits. Profits are obtained from the most efficient methods of production coupled with thorough marketing and the maximum price the market will bear ...' This is a natural and reasonable line of thought. But if one were to challenge, 'Po to make profits' then one would be able to explore other possible developments. 'A business has the social function of providing an environment in which people can make the maximum contribution to society through productivity.'

'A business exists as an efficient production unit. Efficiency is the main aim not profit.'

'A business only exists as an evolutionary stage in the organization of production and its only justification is historical.'

If PO is used skilfully it can divert the line of thought into new pathways by blocking the old ones at certain crucial points. PO is an excuse for choosing a line of thought that is not the most obvious or the best.

● PO and overreaction

The general function of PO is as a laxative to relax the rigidity of a particular way of looking at things. In certain situations a rigid way of looking at things can lead to emotional overreaction. In such cases PO acts as a laugh or a smile to release the tension that accompanies a rigid point of view. Both a laugh and a smile occur when a particular way of looking at a situation is suddenly turned round. PO suggests the possibility of such a change in view. PO acts to lessen the fierce necessity of a particular point of view.

General function of PO

PO is the laxative of language and thinking. PO is the device for carrying out lateral thinking.

PO is a symbol which draws attention to the pattern making behaviour of mind which tends to establish rigid patterns. PO draws attention to the possibility of clichés and rigid ways of looking at things. PO draws attention to the possibility of insight restructuring to obtain new patterns without any further information. Even if PO is never used except as a reminder of these things then it can still be extremely useful.

When used as a practical language tool the function of PO is to indicate that lateral thinking is being used. PO indicates that the arrangement of information being made makes sense from a lateral thinking point of view even if it does not make sense otherwise. Without some definite indicator such as PO there would be confusion when lateral thinking was introduced in the middle of an ordinary vertical thinking discussion.

PO is not a selective device but a generative one. PO is never a judgement. PO never examines why an arrangement of information has been made but looks forward to what effect it may have. PO does not oppose or counteract judgements but merely sidesteps them. PO also protects arrangements of information from judgement.

PO is essentially a device to enable one to use information in a way that is other than the most obvious and the most reasonable. PO allows one to make arrangements of information for which there is no justification. PO also allows one to challenge arrangements of information for which there is full justification.

PO may seem a perversion designed to upset the highly useful system of logical thinking, permanent concepts and the pursuit of the most obvious. PO is not however a perversion but an escape. It does not destroy the usefulness of this system but adds to it by overcoming the rigidity which is the main limitation of the system. It is a *holiday* from the usual conventions of logic not an attack upon them. Without the stabilizing background of traditional vertical thinking PO would not be much use. If everything was chaos then there would be no rigidity to escape from nor would there be any possibility of establishing a more up to date pattern which is what insight is about. As a device PO actually enhances the effectiveness of vertical thinking by keeping it intact. This PO does by providing a means to bypass vertical thinking in order to introduce a generative factor. Once a new pattern has emerged it can be developed with the full rigour of vertical thinking and judged.

Similarity of PO to other words

It may be felt that some of the functions of PO are very similiar to those carried out by such words as hypothesis, possible, suppose and poetry. There are some functions of PO which are indeed similar, for instance the semicertainty function. But there are other functions of PO which are quite different, for instance the juxtaposition of totally unrelated material. Hypothesis, possible and suppose are very weak relations of PO. They cover arrangements of information which seem very reasonable but cannot quite be proved. They are tolerable guesses at the best arrangement of information at the moment. PO in contrast allows information to

be used in ways which are *totally* unreasonable. The most important difference is that with these words the information is used for
its own sake even if the use is tentative. With PO however the
information is not used for its own sake but for its effect.
Perhaps the most similar word is poetry where words are used
not so much for their own meaning as for their stimulating
effect.

The mechanism of PO

Why should PO work? PO could never work in a linear system
like a computer because the arrangement of information in such a
system is always the best possible one according to the programme. But in a self-maximizing system or a system with
humour the arrangement of information into patterns depends
very heavily on the sequence of arrival of information. Thus A
followed by B, followed by C, followed by D, would give a different pattern to B followed by D, followed by A, followed by C.
But if A, B, C and D were all to arrive together then the best
arrangement of them would be different from either of the other
two arrangements. There is a tremendous continuity in this type
of system and this means that it is easy to add to patterns or
combine them but very difficult to restructure them.* There are
also the inherited patterns which are acquired ready made from
other minds.

Because of this tendency to establish patterns and for them to
become ever more rigid one needs a means for disrupting the
patterns in order to let the information come together in new
ways. PO is that means as it is the tool of lateral thinking. PO is
needed because of the behaviour of a self-maximizing memory
system and PO works because of the nature of such a system.
Within such a system some sort of pattern has to form. If the
old pattern is sufficiently dislocated then a new pattern is formed
and the process is insight restructuring.

PO is used to disrupt patterns. PO is used to dislocate patterns.
PO is used as a catalyst to bring together information in a certain

way. From that point on it is the natural behaviour of the mind that snaps the new pattern together. Without such behaviour PO would be useless.

The bigger the change from the old pattern the more likely is a new pattern to snap together. 'Reasonable' arrangements of information are too closely similar to the old arrangements to give new patterns. That is why PO works outside of reason. PO is concerned not with the reason for using information in a certain way but for the effect it will have. Once the new pattern has come about it must of course be judged in the usual way.

In emptying a bucket by a siphon the water must first be sucked upwards in the tube. This is an unnatural direction for water to travel. Once the water has reached a certain position then the siphon forms and the water will continue to flow naturally out of the bucket until it is empty. In the same way an unnatural use of information may be necessary to provoke a rearrangement that is itself perfectly natural.

Grammatical use of PO

PO can be used in any way that seems natural. The most important point is that anything covered by PO should be clearly seen to be covered by PO. The two main functions of PO are first to protect an arrangement of information from judgement and to indicate that it is being used provocatively and second to challenge a particular arrangement of information such as an idea, a concept or a way of putting things. In the second case the material being challenged would be repeated and PO would be added to it. In the other case PO would cover new material.

1. PO as interjection

Here PO would be used by itself as a reply or even as an

interruption much as NO is used. It would imply that a particular way of looking at things was being challenged.
e.g. 'The purpose of sport is to encourage the competitive spirit and the will to win.'
'Po !'
2. PO as preface
Here PO is used before a sentence or a phrase or a word that it is meant to qualify. The qualification may take the form of a challenge or it may take the form of introducing provocative material.
e.g. 'An organization can only function efficiently if all its members show absolute obedience.'
'Po function efficiently.'
or 'Po clockwork with the cogwheels made of rubber.'
3. PO as a juxtaposition
When two words are going to be juxtaposed for no reason at all PO is used to indicate this relationship between them. This same use of PO is involved in the introduction of a random word into a discussion.
e.g. 'Travel po ink.'
or 'Po kangaroos.'
4. PO in the same positions as NO or NOT
PO can be used in any position in which NO or NOT could be used. In such a position PO would qualify exactly the same things as NO or NOT would qualify.
e.g. 'Wednesday is po a holiday.'
In practice it is probably best to try to use PO always at the beginning of a sentence or phrase or right in front of the word to be qualified. PO does not have to be written in capital letters but until one is well used to it capital letters are preferable. If one is using PO and the other person does not understand its use then this can be most simply explained as follows:
1. Challenge function
PO means you may very well be right but let's try and look at it in another way.
2. Provocative function
PO means I am just saying that to see what it sets off in your mind, to see whether that way of putting things can stimulate any new ideas.

3. Anti-arrogance function

PO means don't be so arrogant, so dogmatic. Don't have such a closed mind.

4. Overreaction

PO simply means, let's cool it. There is no point in getting upset about this.

Practice

PO is the language tool of lateral thinking. The concept and function of lateral thinking is crystallized in the use of PO. If one acquires skill in the use of PO then one has skill in the use of lateral thinking. For this reason practice in the use of PO is extremely important. Learning how to use PO is similar to learning how to use NO. Learning how to use NO is however a gradual process spread over many years. With PO one tries to achieve the same effect in a shorter time. It is much better to go slowly and carefully than to rush ahead and teach only a limited or even incorrect use of PO.

In teaching the use of PO it is far better to suggest the general concept of PO than to define rigidly the situations in which it can be used. Nevertheless one needs to show the practical use of PO in language and not just the theory behind it.

Since PO is the tool of lateral thinking any of the previous practice sessions could be reused with PO as the operative device. It is more useful however to devise special situations which indicate the function of PO more specifically.

In this section several aspects of the function of PO have been listed. These aspects can be mentioned in the course of explaining the nature of PO and as one mentions them one can give and ask for further examples. For the actual practice session it is better to group the functions of PO into a few broad uses than to confuse with the detail of each particular use.

The function of PO involves two basic aspects:

● The use of PO.

● The response to PO.

The response to PO

It is far better to learn the response to PO *before* the use of PO. The reason for this apparently paradoxical arrangement is that by learning how to respond to PO one actually learns the reason for using it. In addition by learning the response first one can then practise the use of PO in a more realistic way since it will not only be used but also responded to.

The points about the response to PO are as follows:

1. PO is never a judgement. This means that when PO is used to challenge something that you have said this does not imply disagreement or even doubt. PO is *never met* with a defence of what has been said. Nor is PO met with an exasperated, 'How else could it be put – how would *you* put it?' Furthermore PO is not an indication that the person saying it has a better alternative or even an alternative at all. What PO implies is, 'Without disagreeing with what you say let us – both of us – try and put things together in a different way. It is not me against you but a joint search for an alternative structuring.' It is important to stress this aspect of the *joint search*. It is important to stress that PO is not part of the antagonism of an argument. So one responds to PO by trying to generate alternatives *not* by irritation or by defending the original way of putting things.

2. PO may involve the provocative use of information. This means that information may be put together in a fantastic and completely unjustified way which is covered by PO. In responding to this use of PO one does not argue that the arrangement of information is unacceptable. One does not demand the reason for putting things together in this way. Nor does one sit back and imply, 'Very well, if you want to put things like that you go ahead and show that it can be useful.' The provocative use of PO is to provide a stimulus which is to be used cooperatively by both parties. It implies: 'If we use this arrangement of information as a stimulus what can we both come up with?' So the response to the provocative use of PO is neither condemnation nor indifference but active cooperation.

3. PO may be used as a protection. This means that PO may be used to hold off judgement or to temporarily override a judgement that has resulted in a rejection. The response to this use of PO is *not to show that the judgement is necessary and should be applied at once*. Nor is the response one of exasperation, 'If you won't accept the ordinary uses of right and wrong how can we ever proceed?' Nor is the response one of superior indifference, 'If you want to say that black is white and to play around with that idea for a while I shall just wait until you are through.' As before the proper response is a cooperative exploration of the new situation.

4. PO may be a relaxation. This means that when a situation has become tense through the development of rigid points of view and possibly overreactions, PO is suggested as a smile to relax the tension and to relax the rigid points of view. Here the only appropriate response is to respond with PO (with a mental shrug and a smile) and to relax the rigidity of the situation.

5. PO may be used ambiguously. There are times when it is not clear how PO is being used or what concept is being challenged. In such cases one simply asks for the person using PO either to be more specific or to agree that he really wants to use it in a general way.

In summary one may say that the most important aspect of the response to PO is to realize that it is not directed against anything but is a suggestion for cooperative attempts to restructure a situation. If one feels competitive then one can express this by using PO more effectively than the person suggesting it: that is to say one goes on to generate more alternatives than he does. PO may be an invitation to a race but never an invitation to a conflict.

The use of PO

For convenience the many uses of PO may be divided into three broad classes:

1. The generation of alternatives. Anti-arrogance. Relaxation. Reexamination of a concept. Rethinking. Restructuring.

Indicating an awareness of the possibility of clichés or a rigid point of view.

2. Provocation. The use of arrangements of information as stimuli. Juxtapositions. Introduction of random words. Abolition of concept divisions. The use of fantasy and nonsense.

3. Protection and rescue. Holding off judgement. Temporarily reversing judgement. Removal of the NO label.

The generation of alternatives

PO is used to point out that a particular way of looking at a situation is only one view among many. PO is used to point out that a particular point of view appears to be held with an unjustified arrogance. The first level is merely to suggest that there may be other ways of looking at the situation. This is especially so when one uses PO as an anti-arrogance device.

The next level is to invite restructuring of the situation. Here one asks for alternatives and goes on to supply them oneself.

PO may be applied to a whole idea, a whole sentence, a phrase, a concept or just a word.

Practice

1. The teacher asks a student (a particular student or a volunteer) to talk on some subject. The subject could be something like the following:
What is the use of space travel?
Should all medical aid be free?
Are straight roads better than winding ones?
In the course of the student's talk the teacher interrupts with PO. The interruption repeats part of what the student has said and prefaces it with PO. The student is not expected to respond to PO at this stage. This is explained to him. He just pauses while the teacher interrupts and then carries on.

2. The teacher talks about a subject and this time the students are invited to interrupt with PO in the same way as the teacher

had done in the preceding practice session. Subjects for discussion might include:

The usefulness of different languages.

Whether large organizations work better than small ones.

Was it easier to work alone or in a group?

Each time a student interrupts with PO the teacher responds by generating alternative ways of putting things and the students are encouraged to do the same. For example, a discussion might go something like this:

TEACHER: Different languages are useful because they allow the development of different cultures and so provide more interest.

STUDENT: PO provide more interest.

TEACHER: Different cultures mean different ways of looking at life, different habits and ways of behaving, different art etc. All these are things one can learn about and find out about and compare to one's own. New patterns to be explored. Something to be done.

STUDENT: Different ways of expressing the same thing – they could be useful, they could be a waste of time.

TEACHER: Because of the different language communication is poor and so distinctness emerges instead of a general uniformity.

STUDENT: PO communication is poor.

TEACHER: People cannot talk easily to people with another language or read their books. People cannot influence each other so much.

STUDENT: People cannot influence each other. That may be a bad thing because from such interaction might come better understanding.

TEACHER: PO understanding.

STUDENT: They would know what the other person meant, what he was up to, what he wanted, what his values were.

3. It is quite likely that a discussion of this sort would very quickly become a two way discussion. If not then the teacher can deliberately arrange for a debate type discussion between two students. Each of them is allowed to use PO and so is the teacher who can interrupt with PO but is not allowed to take part in the discussion otherwise.

Comment

In this type of discussion it may become obvious that PO is being used mainly as a focusing device to indicate: 'explain what you mean by ...' or, 'define that ...' or, 'elaborate that point ...' If this seems to be the case then the teacher points out that the function of PO is to ask for a restructuring, to ask for *alternative* ways of putting things. When PO is next used the teacher calls for a pause and then invites the entire class to list different ways of putting whatever has been qualified by PO. For instance 'Po understanding' from the example given above might rise to the following:

Supposing that the other person reacts in the same way as you.

Things mean the same to the other person as to you

Lessen the possibility of misunderstanding.

Full sympathy.

Communication without interpreters or intermediaries.

Ability to listen and respond.

None of these are complete or even very good definitions of 'understanding' but they are different ways of putting things. Perhaps the best of them is 'lessen the possibility of misunderstanding'. This may seem a tautology but from an information point of view it says a great deal.

4. Picture interpretation. This is similar to the picture interpretation that was practised in an earlier session. The caption is removed from a photograph and a student (or students if there are enough copies of the photograph or other means for making it visible to all) is asked to interpret it. He offers an interpretation and then the teacher replies, 'Po'. This simply means, 'Very well. Go on. Generate another alternative. What else could it mean?'

This is a very simple use of PO but it is helpful to practise it since it indicates the use of PO in a much clearer manner than do the other situations.

Provocation

This second use of PO simply indicates that the arrangement of information has no justification except the possibility that it might set off new lines of thought. Such an arrangement of information may be as fantastic or unreasonable as anyone can make it. The arrangement is not examined in itself but only in terms of what it sets off.

5. Juxtaposition. This is the simplest provocative arrangement of information. Two words are put together with PO inserted between them to indicate why they are put together. The pairs of words are then offered to the class one at a time. The session may be conducted in an open class with students volunteering suggestions which are listed by the teacher on a blackboard or else by some student who is asked to take notes. Alternatively the students can list their own ideas and these are collected and compared at the end.

Possible pairs of words might include:

Ice cream po electric light.
Horse po caterpillar.
Book po policeman.
Rain po Wednesday.
Stars po football.
Stars po decision.
Shoe po food.

The students are not specifically asked to relate the words, or to find some connection between the two or to show what the two words have in common. Any sort of ideas at all that arise are accepted. There is no question of directing the sort of ideas that the students ought to be having. If on reading through the results one cannot see the connection then one asks how it came about, one asks for the missing links. One does not care what the idea is but one does want to know how it came about.

6. Random word. This technique has been discussed in a previous chapter. It consists of introducing into the consideration

of a subject a word which has no connection with the subject at all. The idea is to see what the random word triggers off. In this case PO would be used to introduce the random word. An alternative way of doing it would be to take some word which appeared to be vital in the discussion and couple it in juxtaposition with a random word by means of PO.

Possible subjects for discussion might include:

Advantages of saving against spending.
Advantages of attack rather than defence in sport.
Knowing where to find information.
Why do fights start?
Should people do exactly what they want to?
The design of shoes.

Possible random words might include:

Fishing line.
Bus ticket.
Motor car horn.
Eggcup.

7. Concept reuniting. PO can be used to put together again things that have been divided up into separate concepts. PO can be used to remove labels and extract information from pigeonholes. In order to put across this function of PO one takes concepts which have been created by a division (or which have created each other by implication) and puts them together by means of PO. Such paired concepts are presented to the class in the same way as juxtapositions were presented and the ideas arising from this presentation are examined and compared. In this instance it is better if the students individually list their ideas so that when these are read out at the end they can appreciate the usefulness of the procedure.

Possible examples might include:

Soldiers po civilians.
Flexible po rigid.
Attacker po defender.
Order po chaos.
Liquid po solid.
Teacher po student.
Up po down.

Day po night.
North po south.
Right po wrong.
Male po female.

8. In addition to reacting to the juxtapositions and paired concepts provided for them the students can be asked to generate their own juxtapositions and paired concepts. Suggestions for these are collected on slips of paper and then a selection of these is fed back to the students for their reaction. The simple exercise of generating such juxtapositions and paired concepts *is itself* very useful in making clear this particular use of PO.

Protection and rescue

This function of PO is used to delay judgement. In effect it is used to delay rejection for that is the only sort of judgement which would remove an idea from consideration. PO may be used to protect an idea before it has been judged or it may be used to bring back into consideration an idea which has already been judged and rejected. In practice PO is attracted by the NO label. Whenever the NO label is used it is a direct indication of the current frame of reference against which every judgement must be made. By temporarily overriding the rejection with PO one is really reexamining the frame of reference itself.

9. A discussion is started between two students or between the teacher and a student. The discussion continues until either one or the other uses a NO rejection. At that point PO is used to overcome the rejection and the rejected statement is considered in itself to see what ideas it can trigger off.

Possible subjects for discussion might include:
Should people be encouraged to live in the country or in towns?
Does a welfare state encourage people to be lazy?
Is changing fashion in clothes a good thing?
How much should one do for oneself and how much should one pay other people to do for one?
Are classroom lessons too long?

A discussion might go something as follows:

TEACHER: People should be encouraged to live in the country because towns are not healthy.

STUDENT: Towns are not healthy. PO towns are healthy. Towns could be healthy with better planning and better traffic control. Perhaps towns could be more healthy mentally because of more social interaction.

TEACHER: Towns would have better health services because they would be more centralized and communication would be better.

10. A subject is selected and the students are asked to think of all the negative things they can say about that subject. These are listed and then some of them are reexamined using PO. Quite obviously the number of negative things one can say about something is infinite. For instance about an apple one could say: 'It is not black. It is not purple. It is not mauve etc. It is not an orange. It is not a tomato etc.' In practice one would simply ignore that sort of list or pick out of it certain items. For instance 'An apple is not a tomato' could lead to the following idea: 'In some languages the word for tomato is derived from that for apple. In Italian a tomato is called a golden apple. In Sweden the word for an orange is derived from the word for an apple.' To avoid this sort of thing it is probably better to deal with abstract concepts or with functions rather than objects.

Possible subjects might include:

Work.
Freedom.
Duty.
Truth.
Obedience.
Boredom.

General comment on the use of PO

After the initial practice sessions in which the use of PO is obviously excessive and artificial one moves on to the more natural use of PO in ordinary discussion sessions. It is up to the teacher to use PO now and again to indicate how it should be used. The other important point is to watch how the students react to PO when it is used either by other students or by the teacher himself. An inappropriate reaction to PO indicates that the function of PO has not been understood. It is more important to emphasize the correct *reaction* to PO than the correct *use* of it. Someone who knows how to react appropriately to PO will also know how to use it appropriately.

The one sided use of PO

PO is a device for use in one's own thinking and reacting as well as in communication with other people. In fact it is probably of more use in enabling one to use lateral thinking oneself than in allowing the use of lateral thinking in group discussions. This *private* use of PO obviously does not depend on other people understanding its function. In communication however it may come about that one person uses PO and the other person has no idea what it means. In that case one does not desist from using PO but explains what it means. Simple ways of explaining what PO means have been described earlier in this chapter. If in difficulty one could always say that it was a special form of 'suppose'.

Summary

PO is a language device with which to carry out lateral thinking. PO is an insight tool since it enables one to use information in a way that encourages escape from the established patterns and insight restructuring into new ones. PO performs a special function that it is impossible to perform adequately in language without PO. Other ways of carrying out this function are cumbersome, weak and ineffective. The more skill and practice one invests in the use of PO the more effective it becomes. It is not language that makes PO necessary but the mechanism of mind.

I knew the town quite well but I had to ask for instructions as to how to get to this particular restaurant. The instructions were easy to follow as the route was made up of three segments with each of which I was familiar for each of them involved some obvious landmark. The segments had been made familiar by ordinary driving around the town. One day some friends set out for the restaurant from the same place as myself and at the same time. But they got there long before I did. I asked them if they had driven quickly but they denied this. Then I asked them what route they had taken. They explained and it was obvious that they had taken a short cut as shown below.

A small side turning had led them directly to the restaurant while I was making an unnecessary detour through the centre of the town. My own route had always seemed satisfactory so I had never looked for a shorter one. Nor had I ever been aware that there was a shorter one. I had driven past the small side turning each time but had never explored it because there had been no reason to explore it. And without exploring it I could never have found out how useful it was. My original instructions had been in terms of large well-known segments of route, cliché segments, because that is the easiest way to give instructions. There had never been any reason to break off along one of these cliché segments. There are three ways in which thinking can be blocked. These three ways are shown diagrammatically.

1. One is blocked by a gap. One cannot proceed further because the road runs out. One needs to find more road or to construct a bridge across the river. This is equivalent to having to look around for more information or having to generate some by experiment.

2. One is blocked by there being something in the way. Here there is a definite obstacle which bars progress. In order to go on one has to find a way of removing the obstacle or getting round it. Once this has been done progress is easy because the road is there. One can concentrate one's problem solving efforts on overcoming the block.

3. One is blocked because there is nothing in the way. The road is smooth and clear and so one goes shooting past the important side turning unaware that it is even there. Here a particular way of looking at things leads one straight past a better

way of looking at them. Because the first way is adequate one does not even consider that there might be another way – let alone look for it.

This third type of block is what happens when one is blocked by the adequate, blocked by openness. Trying to avoid this sort of block is what lateral thinking is all about. Instead of proceeding with the patterns that have been established on the memory surface of mind one tries to find short cuts to restructure the patterns. Like the route in the restaurant story the established patterns have been constructed out of familiar cliché segments. Even when the patterns are adequate this cannot exclude there being very much more effective patterns.

If things are put together in a certain way to give one pattern then this prevents them being put together in another way to give a different pattern. One way of arranging the three pieces shown overleaf excludes the other way. There is an exclusivity about patterns. Nevertheless a satisfactory pattern cannot preclude the possibility of there being a different and better arrangement. The trouble is that the different and better arrangement does not arise from the current pattern but arises instead of it. There is no logical reason to look for a better way of doing something if there is already an adequate way. Adequate is always good enough. It is interesting that in our thinking we have developed methods for dealing with things that are wrong but no methods for dealing with things that are right. When something is wrong we explore further. When something is right our thinking comes to a halt. That is why we need lateral thinking to break through this adequacy block and restructure patterns even when there is no need to do so.

The difficulty with being blocked by openness is that there is no indication as to where the block has occurred. It might have occurred anywhere along the apparently correct pathway. Two types of branching pattern are shown on p. 235. In the first type there is a definite change of direction at each branch point. One has either to go right or left. This means that one is always *aware* of the branch points. In the second type of branching pattern the branches stem off a straight trunk. If you go along the main pathway you may not even be aware that there was a side branch or a choice point. One is blocked by the openness of the main pathway.

If one comes to a dead end in the first type of branching system one goes back to the branch point and tries the other branch. This can be done again and again for each branch point. But in the second type of branching pattern when one comes to a dead end one cannot just go back to the preceding branch point because one does not even know where the branch points are since one has never had to pause and make a choice at them.

Cliché patterns strung together constitute the trunk of a

straight branching system. As one proceeds smoothly along them one is not even aware that there are possible side turnings. So when one comes to a dead end one does not know where to go.

A plastic piece is shown overleaf. Another plastic piece is provided and the task is to arrange them both together to give a simple shape that would be easy to describe. The arrangement is obvious as shown. A further piece is added and once again the arrangement is obvious. When a fourth piece is added there is difficulty in fitting them all together. The original placing of the second piece so that it nestled in the angle of the first piece is such an obvious pattern that it becomes a cliché. And as a cliché one wants to use it, not disrupt it. This makes the final solution difficult since the small piece has to be placed in quite a different position.

Cliché patterns are satisfactory established patterns which are very useful and which do a good job. They can be used in three ways:

1. For communication. It is easier to explain a situation in terms of cliché patterns than to devise new patterns.

2. One picks out a cliché pattern more easily than other patterns from an environment that offers several alternative patterns.

3. Given only part of a pattern one elaborates this part to a whole pattern – but a cliché whole.

I was having lunch one day in a university cafeteria when I noticed sitting at another table a student with very long hair and a delicate, sensitive face. As I looked at the student I thought to

myself that here was a person whose sex could not be determined by appearance. It was several minutes before I suddenly noticed that the student had a long straggling moustache! In my mind I had gone at once from the long hair and delicate face to the assumption that the student might be a girl and so I had never noticed the moustache. So it is in picking out cliché patterns that one is not even aware that alternative patterns could just as easily have been picked out.

If an ordinary letter is partially hidden under a piece of paper one elaborates the pattern to give the standard letter. Letters are cliché patterns and one only needs a hint in order to be able to elaborate the rest of the letter. It is easy enough to recognize letters in this way because one knows all the possibilities to begin with and also one knows that the pattern must be a letter. But suppose the patterns were not all letters but completely different patterns which were covered up so that the exposed bits did look like letters? One would elaborate the expected cliché pattern and one would be wrong. Or suppose that one did not know the shape of all the letters? The same thing would happen. In real life one

is always elaborating patterns as if they could only be standard cliché patterns.

This process of being blocked by openness is very prevalent in thinking. In a way it is the basis of thinking for thinking has to make guesses and assumptions based on past experience. Useful as it is, the process has definite disadvantages especially in terms of new ideas and of bringing patterns up to date. This process of being blocked by openness is at the very centre of the need for lateral thinking. Lateral thinking is an attempt to find alternative pathways, an attempt to put things together in a new way, no matter how adequate the old way appears to be.

Practice

The sole intention of this practice session is not to practise any technique but to illustrate the phenomenon of being blocked by openness. This is done by showing how easy it is to be satisfied by what seems to be a satisfactory explanation.

1. Stories, anecdotes, jokes. The students are invited to think of examples of the process of being blocked by adequacy. The examples may be from their own experience or else incidents they have heard about. The teacher can note down these incidents and add them to his own stockpile of material for future occasions. In any case the teacher may already have collected examples of this sort and can use them to illustrate what is wanted.

e.g. I had a guest staying in my house. After the guest had left I found that the reading lamp would not work. I checked the bulb and I checked the fuse but still the lamp would not work. I was just about to dismantle the plug when it occurred to me that the guest might have switched off the lamp by the switch on the lamp base and not the wall switch which is what I usually did. This in fact was what had happened.

2. The students are shown parts of a picture or else a picture with parts obscured by a cardboard sheet. They are asked to decide what the picture is all about. They are encouraged to jump to conclusions before the rest of the picture is revealed.

3. The use of blanks. The students are asked to write a short passage on some theme and then to go over the passage striking out any word which would make the theme obvious. The passage is then rewritten with 'blank' substituted for such words. Alter-

natively the students can just write the passage and then the teacher strikes out the revealing words and puts 'blank' instead. A third way to do it is to take a passage from a newspaper and magazine and treat it in the same way. It is best to give the students an example of what is wanted before asking them to provide such passages. The blanked out passage is then read out to the rest of the students who are asked firstly to decide what the passage is about and then to try to fill in the individual blanks. This is done as an individual effort by each student and at the end the results are compared.

An example of this sort of passage might be: 'He stood by the side of *blank* and every time a *blank* approached he would raise his arm and *blank*. It was some time before he eventually got *blank* and even so that did not take *blank*.'

In this passage the *blank* refers to anything that has been left out. It is important to point out that this need not apply to a single word but could be used for a group of words. Thus the phrase, 'get anywhere' would be replaced by *blank* just as would be the word 'car'.

The previous section was about being blocked by openness. It dealt with the way adequate established patterns prevented the development of patterns that made better use of the available information. Normally one is only taught to think about things until one gets an adequate answer. One goes on exploring while things are unsatisfactory but as soon as they become satisfactory one stops. And yet there may be an answer or an arrangement of information that is far better than the adequate one. All this is part of the first aspect of lateral thinking. This first aspect is to create an awareness of the limitations of established patterns. Such established patterns can do three things:

1. They can create problems which do not really exist. Such problems are only created by particular divisions, polarizations, conceptualizations.

2. They can act as traps or prisons which prevent a more useful arrangement of information.

3. They can block by adequacy.

This first aspect of lateral thinking is to become aware of the process and the need for it. The second aspect involves developing some skill in the use of lateral thinking.

It is not much use treating lateral thinking as an abstract process. Nor is it much use treating it as something to do with creativity and hence desirable in a general sort of way. Nor is it much use accepting lateral thinking as being of use to some people at some time in some circumstances. Lateral thinking is a necessary part of thinking and it is everybody's business. One needs to go further than awareness and appreciation and to actually practise it. Throughout this book different ways of practising lateral thinking have been suggested. In each case the idea has been to use a specific technique. In addition to such specific practice sessions one needs some general practice situations. In dealing with the general situations one can use the techniques learned elsewhere or one can develop for oneself deliberate habits of mind and deliberate ways of applying lateral thinking.

It would be possible to become involved in some project in depth. In the course of working through such a project there might be opportunity to use lateral thinking. In fact the opportunity to do so would be very small for in a specialized project treated in depth the emphasis is on the collection of specialized knowledge or its application. This is a matter of vertical thinking. Lateral thinking is most used when knowledge is readily available 'and the emphasis is on the *best* use of that knowledge. It is far more useful to practise lateral thinking over a large number of small projects than to suppose that it is practised in the pursuit of a large project.

There are three practical situations which encourage the use of lateral thinking.

- Description.
- Problem solving.
- Design.

Description

An object or a situation may be described by someone in a particular way and by someone else in a different way. There can be as many descriptions as there are points of view. Some descriptions may be more useful than others, some descriptions may be more complete than others. But there is no one description which is correct, leaving all the others to be wrong. That is why description is an easy way of showing how something can be looked at in different ways. It is also an easy way of practising the ability to generate alternative ways of looking at something.

Furthermore when one learns to generate alternative points of view oneself one is ready to appreciate the validity of other people's points of view.

Description is a way of making visible the way one understands something – the way one explains that thing to oneself. By having to describe something one has to commit oneself temporarily to a particular point of view. This means that one has to generate a definite point of view instead of being satisfied with a vague awareness.

The idea of this exercise is to train people to realize that there is more than one way of looking at a situation and to be able to generate alternative ways for themselves. For this reason the emphasis is not on the accuracy of the description but on the *difference* between descriptions and on the use of novel methods of description.

The raw material which is to be described may be picture material. This could take the form of photographs or ready made pictures or the students could be asked to draw pictures themselves for the others to describe. Simple geometric outline shapes are a good way to start. One can move on from visual material to written material. With written material one is really redescribing something that has already been described. It may be a story, an account from a book or a newspaper article. Real life situations can be identified by name without describing them just as real life objects can be identified and then the full description is left to the students. For instance students could be asked to describe a harvesting machine or the parliamentary system. Acting as in charades could also be the object of description. Obviously there is no limit to what can be described.

The descriptions may be verbal or written or even in picture form. Once they have been obtained the emphasis is on showing the different approaches. Students are encouraged to find still further approaches.

Although one is not interested in finding the best possible description one still needs to bear in mind what is a useful description and what is not. The material to be described is not being used as a stimulus to set off ideas. The task is not to generate ideas which have something to do with the material but to describe that material. The best criterion of adequate description is as follows:

'Suppose you had to describe this scene to someone who could not see it, how would you describe it?'

One is not looking for the complete and pedantic description. A description which only conveys one aspect of the material may be very good if it does so vividly. Descriptions may be partial, complete or general.

For instance in describing a geometric square the following descriptions may be offered:

A figure which has four equal sides.

A figure which has only four angles and all of them are right angles.

A rectangle with all the sides being equal.

If you walk north for two miles then turn sharply east and continue for two miles, then sharply south and continue for two more miles, then sharply west and continue for two more miles, the path of your walk looked at from an aeroplane would be a square.

If you take a rectangle which is twice as long as it is broad, and cut it in half straight down the middle you would have two squares.

If you put together two right-angled isosceles triangles, base to base, you would have a square.

Some of the above descriptions are obviously very incomplete. Others are very roundabout.

Description is certainly the easiest setting in which to practise lateral thinking because there is always some result.

Problem solving

Like description problem solving is a format that has been used in the suggested practice sessions throughout this book. A problem is not just an artificially arranged difficulty that is only to be found in textbooks. A problem is simply the difference between what one has and what one wants. Any question poses a problem.

Generating and solving problems is the basis of forward thinking and progress. If description is a matter of looking back to see what one has then problem solving is a matter of looking forward to see what one can get.

In any problem there is a desired end point – something one wants to bring about. What one wants to bring about may take a variety of forms:

1. To resolve some difficulty (traffic congestion problem).
2. To bring about something new (design an apple picking machine).
3. To do away with something unsatisfactory (road accidents, starvation).

All these are but different aspects of the same process which is to bring about a change in the state of affairs. For instance the traffic congestion problem could be phrased in three ways:

1. To resolve the difficulty of traffic congestion.
2. To design a road system which would have free traffic flow.
3. To get rid of the frustration and delay of traffic congestion.

Problems may be open ended or closed. Most of the problems used in this book are open ended problems. This is because it would be impossible to have the time or the facilities for trying out solutions to a variety of real life problems. With open ended problems one can only offer suggestions as to how the problem might be solved. Since these suggestions cannot actually be tried out to see if they work they have to be judged in some other way. Judgement is based on what one thinks would happen if the solution was actually tried out. It may be the teacher who makes the judgement or the other students. The emphasis, however, is not on judging the suggested solutions but on generating different approaches. Where possible one acknowledges a suggestion and even elaborates it rather than reject it. The only time one has to enforce judgement is when the suggestions wander so far from the problem that one is no longer trying to solve it at all. Though a problem may in fact be solved by information generated in another context the purpose of this type of problem-solving practice is to try to solve the given problem.

With closed problems there is a definite answer. The solution either works or it does not. There may be only one solution but more often there are alternative solutions. Some of these solutions may be better than others but for this purpose it is enough that the solution works. It is better to find a variety of solutions than to only find the best one. Closed problems have to be fairly simple because they have to be capable of being solved in a simple setting. Alternatively one has to have a notational system like mathematics which permits one to make one's own model of the real world. It is better however to keep away from purely mathematical problems since these require knowledge of technique. There are various verbal problems which have verbal solutions. Some of them involve the simplest of mathematics but the solution really depends on the way the problem is looked at. (e.g. There was a line of ducks walking along and there were two ducks in front of a duck and two ducks behind a duck. How many ducks were there? The answer is three ducks). One can build up a stock of such problems by noting them down whenever one comes across them. It is very important that none of the problems depends on verbal tricks for the students must not be given the impression that the teacher is out to *trick* them by means of puns and so on.

A useful type of problem is the artificial mechanical problem of the closed type. Such problems deal with actual objects, for instance how to get a long ladder through a short room. It is possible to generate such problems deliberately by taking a simple straightforward activity and then making a problem of it by severely limiting the starting position. For instance the problem might be: 'How would you empty a glass of water if you are not allowed to lift it off the table?' Another such problem might be: 'How could you carry three pints of water in a newspaper?' When using this type of problem one must be extremely careful in defining the starting position. One cannot go back afterwards and say that something was assumed or taken for granted. For instance if you ask students to cut a postcard into a certain shape then you cannot say: 'But I did not say you could fold the card', or 'It was assumed you could not fold the card otherwise it would be too easy.' This point is important because if you tell students to make assumptions and presume boundaries in their problem solving then you are going directly against the purpose of lateral thinking which challenges the limiting effect of such assumptions.

pute246 Lateral Thinking

Many of these artificial closed problems may seem rather trivial. But this does not matter for the processes used in solving such problems can be isolated and transferred to other problems. The idea is to develop a repertoire of problem solving processes.

There is a third type of problem which can be used in the classroom situation but it involves the teacher doing some homework. The idea is to put forward problems that have already been solved but to withhold the solution. The teacher has to imagine how the problem might have been stated before the solution was found. The situations must of course be ones with which the students are not familiar. For instance students might be asked: 'How would you make plastic buckets or plastic tubing?' The teacher who would know about moulds, vacuum forming, extrusion etc would encourage suggestions and give the answer at the end. It is sometimes as well to ask if anyone already knows the answer because if so he can be told to keep quiet or to explain the answer himself at the end. If the students each write out their own suggestions there is no danger of the problem being spoiled by someone who knows the answer. This sort of problem can be generated by using one's imagination, by reading magazines (science, technology etc) or by wandering around exhibitions. There is no harm in reinventing things that have already been invented. It is very good practice.

Design

Design is really a special case of problem solving. One wants to bring about a desired state of affairs. Occasionally one wants to remedy some fault but more usually one wants to bring about something new. For that reason design is more open ended than problem solving. It requires more creativity. It is not so much a matter of linking up a clearly defined objective with a clearly defined starting position (as in problem solving) but more a matter of starting out from a general position in the direction of a general objective.

A design does not have to be a drawing but for the practice of lateral thinking it is much more useful if the design always takes the form of a drawing. It does not matter how good the drawing is so long as there is an attempt to give a visual description of what is meant.

Explanatory notes may be added to the drawing but they must be brief. The advantage of a drawing is that there is far more commitment than with a verbal explanation. Words can be very general but a line has to be put in a definite place. For instance in the design of a potato peeling machine it would be easy to say, 'The potatoes go in there and then they get washed.' But when this is described visually one can get the effect shown on p. 250. The designer wanted to use a bucket of water to wash the potatoes and the best way to fit the bucket into his machine was by turning it on its side – so the water level had to be turned on its side as well. This beautiful cliché use of the bucket of water would never have been apparent in a purely verbal description.

● Comparison

The first purpose of the design exercise is to show that there are alternative ways of carrying out some function. A single designer will only be able to see one or perhaps a few alternative ways of doing something. But with a large number of designers there will be a large number of alternative approaches. Thus by simply exposing any single designer to the efforts of the others one shows how it is possible to look at things in different ways. The object of the design session is not to teach design but to teach lateral thinking – to teach the ability to generate alternative ways of looking at something.

In practice some general design theme is given to the class (apple picking machine, cart to go over rough ground, potato peeling machine, cup that does not spill, redesigning the human body, redesigning a sausage, redesigning an umbrella, a machine to cut hair etc). The students are asked to come up with designs for the particular design task set. To make comparison easier it is best to only set *one design project* rather than let the students select their own from a list. The individual designs are then collected and compared.

The comparisons may refer to the whole design (e.g. picking the apples off a tree as compared to shaking the tree) or to some particular function (e.g. grabbing the apples with a mechanical hand as compared to sucking them through a hole).

● Cliché units

In examining the submitted designs one very quickly becomes aware of cliché units. Cliché units are standard ways of doing something that are borrowed entire from another setting. For instance a bucket and water to wash potatoes in is a cliché unit. The second purpose of the design exercise is to point out these standard ways of doing things and to show how they may not be the best way.

In pointing out the cliché units one does not judge them. Certainly one does not condemn them for being cliché units. In the design process one has to go through cliché units before moving on to something more appropriate. One merely points out the cliché unit and encourages the designer to go further.

The entire design may be a cliché unit. Thus when children were asked to design a cart to go over rough ground one boy drew a warlike tank complete with cannon, machine guns and rocket missiles. Such entire cliché units are borrowed directly from films, television, comics, encyclopedias etc.

More often the cliché unit is only part of the design. In the apple picking machine project one student drew a large robot man picking apples off a tree. From the top of the robot's head a wire went to a control switch in the hand of a normal man standing just behind. The large robot was complete down to eyelashes. Another picture showed a boxlike structure with a plain disc for a head. This structure stood on two legs and it was equipped with two simple picking arms each of which had five fingers. Another design had done away with the legs and converted the disclike head into a dial with a pointer showing 'fast ... faster ... stop'; but the two arms with five fingers were retained. A further design did away with the head but kept the arms. Finally a very sophisticated design showed a small mobile wheeled car with a long arm that stretched out to the apples. At

This machey go over rough ground.
This is a different kink of bonk
Once bonb too trans. This tank gos over tough ground
There is three men wghtin woking the tank
It will push a rock out the wae.

the end of the arm was a complete hand with five fingers. One
might have supposed this was just a neat way of indicating a
picking function but there was a black hole in the middle of the
hand and an explanatory note, 'Apples are sucked through this
hole.' In this series cliché units ranged from the complete duplicate man to the hand with five useless fingers.

As suggested above one may have to pass through cliché units
in the course of the design process. The cliché units may be
handled in the following ways (among others).

1. Trimming and splitting

A complete cliché unit is taken and then the inessentials are
trimmed away much as one might trim a rosebush. For instance
in a sophisticated design for a potato peeling machine one designer wanted to go further and fry the potatoes to make chips.
So he included a frying pan *complete* with handle. Since the
potatoes were mechanically transported into and out of the pan
the handle was obviously superfluous.

Through repeated trimming one gradually narrows down the
cliché unit to that part which is really necessary. (This is the
whole purpose of that branch of engineering known as Value
Engineering.) Trimming may be a gradual process with a small

Potato mashin

amount removed each time or it may involve large slashes. For instance from the cliché unit of a tank one may slash off all the warlike function and keep only the caterpillar track. Where the jump is very large it may be more a matter of splitting a cliché unit than trimming it. Trimming and splitting are concept breaking procedures and being able to use them is a process of lateral thinking – the escape from rigid patterns.

2. Abstraction and extraction

In a way this is just a form of splitting. To extract the critical part of a cliché unit is the same as splitting off everything else. In practice however the two processes are different. One may either recognize the essential part and remove it (extraction) or one may deal with the cliché unit, trimming off bit after bit until one comes to the essential part.

What is extracted may actually be part of the cliché unit. On the other hand it may be something less tangible, something that depends on looking at the cliché unit in a particular way. For instance one may *abstract* the concept of function. Though the concept is derived from the cliché unit it is not a physical part of it but a particular description. Nevertheless it might not have arisen without the cliché unit. Thus in the apple picking machine 'picking' is an abstracted function that arises directly from the cliché unit of the human hand.

3. Combining

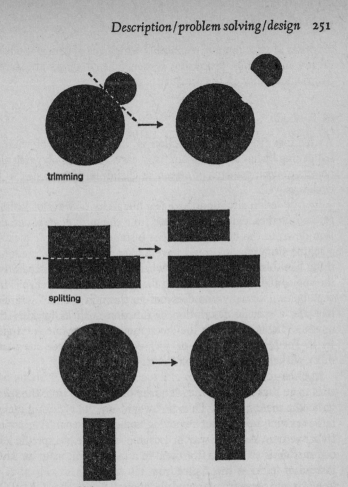

trimming

splitting

combining

Here one takes cliché units from several different sources and puts them together to give a new unit which does not occur anywhere. This process of combination may be by simple addition of function (caterpillar tracks, telescopic arm, hand to pick apples) or there may be some multiplication of function (e.g. for a redesign of the human body: noses on the legs so they would be nearer the ground and be more useful for tracking).

These different ways of handling cliché units cover the basic processes of selection and combining which are of course the basis of any information processing system. The processes are shown diagrammatically on the previous page.

● Function

As distinct from objects function is the description of what is happening, what is going on. It is easy to think of particular objects or arrangements of objects as clichés but functions can be clichés as well.

In any design situation there is a hierarchy of ways of looking at the function. One could proceed from the most general description down to the most specific. For instance in the apple picking machine situation one could have a hierarchy which went something like this: getting apples to where you want them, separating the apples and the tree, removing the apples from the tree, picking the apples. Normally one does not go through such a hierarchy but uses a specific description of function such as 'picking the apples'. The more specific the description the more one is trapped by it. For instance the use of 'picking' would exclude the possibility of shaking the apples off the tree.

In order to escape the trap of a too specific idea of function one tries to go backwards up the hierarchy of function, from the specific to the more general. Thus one would say, 'not picking apples but removing apples, not removing apples but separating apples from the tree'. Another way of escaping from the too specific idea of function is to change it around in a true lateral manner. Thus instead of 'picking the apples from the tree' one would think of 'removing the tree from around the apples'.

When asked to design a cup that would not spill, a group of children showed a variety of functional approaches. The first approach was to design a cup that could not be knocked over. Three possible ways of doing this were suggested: long hands that descended from the ceiling to immobilize the cup; 'sticky material' on the table to attach the cup; a pyramid shaped cup. The second approach was to have a cup that would not spill even when it was knocked over. This was done either by having a special cover to the cup (the cover being flipped open by a catch when one wanted to drink) or by shaping the cup so that the liquid always stayed at the bottom no matter in what position the cup was (rather like unspillable inkwells).

The trouble with function is that once one has decided the particular function then one's design ideas are very much fixed. So one wants to pay attention to generating alternative *functions* and not just ways of carrying out a particular function.

The abstraction of a function is a very useful way of getting ideas moving in the design process. If one is stuck with a particular way of doing something (a hand to pick apples) then one can not get much further. But if one abstracts the function from this particular situation then one can find other ways of carrying out that function. This process is shown in the diagram below. The design results obtained from the students can be compared by showing which designs are but different ways of carrying out the same function. On the other hand one can also show how a different concept of function leads to a completely different approach.

In dealing with function one wants to show two things:

1. How the abstraction of a function can lead to different ways of carrying out this function.

2. How one may need to change a particular idea of function in order to generate new approaches.

In practice one might say: 'That is one way of carrying out this picking function – can you think of any others?' But one might also say: 'Those are different ways of carrying out this picking function but is that the only way of looking at it. Suppose we leave aside the idea of picking and just think of removing the apples from the trees.'

● Design objectives

In a design problem there is very rarely only a single objective. Usually there is a main objective and many subsidiary objectives which may not be apparent. For instance in the design of an apple picking machine the main objective may be to reach and pick the apples but in achieving this objective one may make it impossible to achieve the other objectives as well. Shaking the trees to remove the apples would satisfy the main objective but it would damage the apples. Having a huge machine to do the job might satisfy both the above objectives but might be so uneconomical that it would still be cheaper to do it by hand. Thus three objectives have become apparent: picking the apples, obtaining undamaged apples, a machine that is more economical to use than hand labour. There are other objectives. For instance the machine might have to work at a given speed or it might have to be of such a size that it could pass easily between the trees in a standard orchard. All these objectives might be specified in a description of a desired machine or else they might only become apparent when the design was being examined.

Some designers try to keep all the objectives in mind all the time. They would only move forward very slowly and they would immediately reject an idea that failed to satisfy one of the objectives. Other designers would move quickly ahead in an attempt to satisfy the main objective. Having found some sort of solution they would then look around and see how well the other objectives were satisfied. This second method is probably more generative, but it does depend on a thorough assessment at the end otherwise the effect may be disastrous if one important objective is overlooked. It is better to have this assessment at the end rather than at each stage for an assessment at each stage would prevent the consideration of ideas which were inadequate in themselves, but served as stepping stones to much better ideas.

● Design and lateral thinking

This section is not meant to be a treatise on design but an indication that the design process involves much lateral thinking and provides an excellent setting in which to practise lateral thinking. In the design process one is always trying to restructure concepts; one observes cliché units and tries to get rid of them; one is continually having to generate fresh approaches.

Many of the examples used in this section were obtained from the design efforts of children aged seven to ten years old. Such children are relatively unsophisticated and the design process is a caricature of the design process which would be used by older people. The advantages of such examples are that the design process and its faults are made much more clear. The faults arise from the way the mind handles information and not from any peculiarity of youth. In a less obvious form the same faults occur at all age levels.

The first purpose of the design setting is to get students to generate alternatives. The second purpose is to get them to look beyond the adequate in order to produce something better. The third purpose is to free them from domination by cliché patterns. These three purposes paraphrase the purpose of lateral thinking.

Practice

The students are set a specific design task. Each student tackles the same task. Every design is a drawing. Brief notes may appear on the drawing to indicate how something works. In addition there may be a fuller explanation but this fuller explanation should only refer to what is already in the drawing – it is not to be a substitute for the drawing. Half an hour is enough time to allow for each design project since one is not so interested in the excellence of the design but in the process itself.

When the design task is set some of the students may ask for additional information. For instance if the task was to design a vehicle to go over rough ground then someone could well ask how rough the ground was to be. Though such questions are perfectly legitimate and in a real design situation one would specify the objective very closely, it is better to specify nothing. This means that each student is allowed to assume his own specifications. This gives a much wider variety of response. In discussing the results one can comment on the way the designs fulfil other objectives as well as the main one but one must not condemn a design for not fulfilling a condition which was never given.

The collected results may be discussed there and then or they may be examined and discussed at a subsequent session. Wherever possible it might be an advantage to display the results in some way before discussing them.

As suggested before, the discussion is centred on comparisons of the different ways of doing things and the picking out of cliché units. It is best to avoid making comparisons as to which is the best design for fear of restricting imagination. If one does want to pick out a design as being very good one can do so by commenting on something specific for instance the originality or economy of it rather than giving a blanket approval such as 'good'. Otherwise one uses such comments as 'interesting', 'unusual', 'very different' etc. Above all one wants to refrain from condemning any particular design. Such condemnation can only be restrictive. If one wants to encourage some particular feature one can do so by praising it where it is present rather than condemning its absence. For this reason it is best not to allow students to pass open judgement on the design efforts of others (i.e. not to call for such judgements in the class situation).

Suggestions for design projects have been given in the course of this section. In general the design project may ask for a design to do something that is not done at the moment (e.g. a machine to cut hair), or to do something in a better way (e.g. redesign a comb). The projects may be simple or more complicated. On the whole simple mechanical designs are more useful than abstract ideas. Students may be asked to redesign any everyday object whatsoever, for instance: telephone receiver, pencil, bicycle, stove, shoes, desks. Further suggestions are given in the previous section on design.

● Will it work?

One does not want to restrict designs to the sane, workable ones by carefully analysing each one and rejecting those which would not work. Nevertheless one does want the students to aim for a workable design and not produce a fantasy for the sake of fantasy. The level of mechanical knowledge which one could expect of the students obviously varies with their age but in any case one is not testing this. It is sufficient if every now and again the teacher picks out a design which would obviously not work and gets the class as a whole to accept that it would not work but can still lead to useful ideas. The judgement is not as to whether the design is workable but as to whether the designer was genuinely trying to make a workable design (even if everyone else can see that it would not work). If there is any doubt it is better to say nothing and simply ignore the design.

The emphasis in education has always been on logical sequential thinking which is by tradition the only proper use of information. Creativity is vaguely encouraged as some mysterious talent. This book has been about lateral thinking. Lateral thinking is not a substitute for the traditional logical thinking but a necessary complement. Logical thinking is quite incomplete without lateral thinking.

Lateral thinking makes quite a different use of information from logical (vertical) thinking. For instance the need to be right at every step is absolutely essential to logical thinking but quite unnecessary in lateral thinking. It may sometimes be necessary to be wrong in order to dislocate a pattern sufficiently for it to reform in a new way. With logical thinking one makes immediate judgements, with lateral thinking one may delay judgements in order to allow information to interact and generate new ideas.

The twin aspects of lateral thinking are first the provocative use of information and second the challenge to accepted concepts. Underlying both these aspects is the main purpose of lateral thinking which provides a means to restructure patterns. This restructuring of patterns is necessary to make better use of information that is already available. It is an insight restructuring.

The mind is a pattern making system. The mind creates patterns out of the environment and then recognizes and uses such patterns. This is the basis of its effectiveness. Because the sequence of arrival of information determines how it is to be arranged into a pattern such patterns are always less than the best possible arrangement of information. In order to bring such patterns up to date and so make better use of the contained information one needs a mechanism for insight restructuring. This can never be provided by logical thinking which works to relate accepted concepts not to restructure them. Lateral thinking is demanded by the behaviour of this type of information processing system in order to bring about insight restructuring. The provocative function of lateral thinking and the challenging function are both directed towards this end. In both cases information is used in a manner that goes beyond reason for lateral thinking works outside of reason. Yet the need for lateral thinking is based quite logically on the deficiencies of a self-maximizing memory system which is the type of system that makes the mind capable of humour.

Lateral thinking works at an earlier stage than vertical thinking. Lateral thinking is used to restructure the perceptual pattern which is the way a situation is looked at. Vertical thinking then accepts that perceptual pattern and develops it. Lateral thinking is generative, vertical thinking is selective. Effectiveness is the aim of both.

In ordinary traditional thinking we have developed no methods for going beyond the adequate. As soon as something is satisfactory our thinking must stop. And yet there may be many better arrangements of information beyond the merely adequate. Once one has reached an adequate answer then it is difficult to proceed by logical thinking because the rejection mechanism which is the basis of logical thinking can no longer function well. With lateral thinking one can easily proceed beyond the adequate by insight restructuring.

Lateral thinking is especially useful in problem solving and in the generation of new ideas. But it is not confined to these situations for it is an essential part of all thinking. Without a method for changing concepts and bringing them up to date one is liable to be trapped by concepts which are more harmful than useful. Moreover rigid concept patterns can actually create a great number of problems. Such problems are particularly fierce, since they cannot be altered by available evidence but only by insight restructuring.

The need to change ideas is becoming more and more obvious as technology speeds up the rate of communication and progress. We have never developed very satisfactory methods for changing ideas but have always relied on conflict. Lateral thinking is directed towards bringing about changes in ideas through insight restructuring.

Lateral thinking is directly concerned with insight and with creativity. But whereas both these processes are usually only recognized after they have happened lateral thinking is a deliberate way of using information in order to bring them about. In practice lateral thinking and vertical thinking are so complementary that they are mixed together. Nevertheless it is best to treat them as distinct in order to understand the basic nature of lateral thinking and acquire skill in its use. This also prevents confusion because the principles governing the use of information in lateral thinking are quite different from the ones used in vertical thinking.

It is difficult to acquire any sort of skill in lateral thinking simply by reading about it. In order to develop such skill one must practise and go on practising and that is why there has been such emphasis in this book on practice sessions. Nor are exhortation and goodwill enough. There are specific techniques for the application of lateral thinking. The purpose of such techniques is twofold. They can be used for their own sake but more importantly they can be used to develop the lateral habit of mind.

In order to use lateral thinking effectively one needs a practical language tool. Such a tool is necessary to allow one to use information in the special way required by lateral thinking and also to indicate to others what is being done. This tool is PO. PO is an insight tool. PO is the laxative of language. It acts to relax the rigidity of the tight patterns so easily formed by mind, and to provoke new patterns.

Lateral thinking is not concerned with generating doubt for the sake of doubt or chaos for the sake of chaos. Lateral thinking acknowledges the extreme usefulness of order and of pattern. But it emphasizes the need for changing these to bring them up to date and make them even more useful. Lateral thinking particularly emphasizes the dangers of rigid patterns which the mind is so apt to construct because of the way it handles information.

FOR THE BEST IN PAPERBACKS, LOOK FOR THE 🐧

In every corner of the world, on every subject under the sun, Penguin represents quality and variety – the very best in publishing today.

For complete information about books available from Penguin – including Puffins, Penguin Classics and Arkana – and how to order them, write to us at the appropriate address below. Please note that for copyright reasons the selection of books varies from country to country.

In the United Kingdom: Please write to *Dept E.P., Penguin Books Ltd, Harmondsworth, Middlesex, UB7 0DA.*

If you have any difficulty in obtaining a title, please send your order with the correct money, plus ten per cent for postage and packaging, to *PO Box No 11, West Drayton, Middlesex*

In the United States: Please write to *Dept BA, Penguin, 299 Murray Hill Parkway, East Rutherford, New Jersey 07073*

In Canada: Please write to *Penguin Books Canada Ltd, 2801 John Street, Markham, Ontario L3R 1B4*

In Australia: Please write to the *Marketing Department, Penguin Books Australia Ltd, P.O. Box 257, Ringwood, Victoria 3134*

In New Zealand: Please write to the *Marketing Department, Penguin Books (NZ) Ltd, Private Bag, Takapuna, Auckland 9*

In India: Please write to *Penguin Overseas Ltd, 706 Eros Apartments, 56 Nehru Place, New Delhi, 110019*

In the Netherlands: Please write to *Penguin Books Nederland B.V., Postbus 195, NL–1380AD Weesp*

In West Germany: Please write to *Penguin Books Ltd, Friedrichstrasse 10–12, D–6000 Frankfurt/Main 1*

In Spain: Please write to *Longman Penguin España, Calle San Nicolas 15, E–28013 Madrid*

In Italy: Please write to *Penguin Italia s.r.l., Via Como 4, I-20096 Pioltello (Milano)*

In France: Please write to *Penguin Books Ltd, 39 Rue de Montmorency, F-75003 Paris*

In Japan: Please write to *Longman Penguin Japan Co Ltd, Yamaguchi Building, 2-12-9 Kanda Jimbocho, Chiyoda-Ku, Tokyo 101*

The Use of Lateral Thinking

This is Edward de Bono's original portrayal of a mental process which he in no way claims to have invented. In it he deliberately uses the lateral approach (with intriguing visual examples in one chapter) to sketch in the nature of lateral thinking.

There emerges the concept of an imaginative, free-wheeling, opportunist (but low-probability) mode of thought in which fresh ideas, which may well be simple, sound and effective, are often thrown up. Lateral thinking is thus contrasted with the orthodox, logical, unimaginative (but high-probability) process of vertical thinking, from which it differs as a bus differs from a tram. In a changing world both modes are required.

The Five-Day Course in Thinking

Edward de Bono, originator of 'Lateral Thinking', believes that thinking is an enjoyable skill.

This book offers a series of simple but intriguing problems in thinking that require no special knowledge and no mathematics. The problems are designed to let the reader find out about his own pesonal style of thinking, its weaknesses and strengths, and the methods, latent in himself, that he never uses. Being right is not always important – an error can lead to the right decision.

A copy of the famous L game is inserted in each book for use in the section on strategy. This classic game was designed by de Bono as a basically simple game that can be played with a high degree of skill – and in the process can promote strategic thinking.

BY THE SAME AUTHOR

The Mechanism of Mind

Patterns made by drops of water on different surfaces or by electric bulbs in advertising displays help Dr de Bono, in this fascinating and provocative book, to build up a picture of a 'special memory-surface', which might resemble the brain in its selection, processing and rejection of information. With simple analogies he illustrates the mind's tendency to create and consolidate rigid patterns, to build myths to polarize and divide, and then relates these mechanisms to the various modes of thinking – natural, logical, mathematical and lateral. In conclusion Edward de Bono coins and defines a new word of one syllable, with the startling suggestion that its addition to the language could greatly widen the effectiveness of human thinking.

Po: Beyond Yes and No

NO is the basic tool of the logic system.
YES is the basic tool of the belief system.
PO is the basic tool of the creative system.

Po: Beyond Yes and No is the basic primer of a revolutionary new way of thinking. Edward de Bono maintains that most of us are trapped within the rigid confines of traditional ways of thinking, limited by concepts which have developed simply for the purpose of arriving at the 'right' answer. While humanity has advanced technologically, in the realm of ideas and thought process we are, he says, still using the restricted and resricting concepts that have always been used.